Ethics Engine

Ethics Engine

Building Morality Into Machines

Levent Karaman

Mindful Pages

Published in 2026

ISBN: 9789374126653 (PB)
ISBN: 9789374126295 (eBook)

Published by

Mindful Pages
Imprint of Alpha Editions LLC
312 W. 2nd St #1834
Casper, WY 82601, USA

This book was developed using advanced writing tools to support the drafting and ideation process. All content has been thoughtfully curated, refined, and reviewed to ensure quality and relevance.

Content

Introduction The Machine's Moral Blind Spot viii

Chapter 1 The Problem Is the Specification.........................1

Chapter 2 What We Owe to Each Other (and to Users)...33

Chapter 3 Data, Bias, and the Shape of the World 66

Chapter 4 Causality, Uncertainty, and the Ethics of Not Knowing 96

Chapter 5 Human in the Loop, or Human on the Hook? 124

Chapter 6 Governance That Bites 156

Chapter 7 Culture — The Code You Don't See................187

Chapter 8 Building the Ethics Engine 217

About the Author 250

Introduction
The Machine's Moral Blind Spot

On a cloudless afternoon in Arizona, an autonomous car glides through a suburban street. Sensors hum, code executes, probabilities flicker into motion. A pedestrian steps from the kerb—an ordinary act, banal and foreseeable—and yet, the car brakes a fraction too late. The machine obeys every compliance rule, logs every decision, passes every audit. Its maker declares the system "safe within regulatory thresholds". But the pedestrian is dead. Somewhere between the lines of regulation and the limits of computation, morality fell through the gap.

Elsewhere, a hiring algorithm touts its fairness credentials. It diversifies the shortlist and uplifts underrepresented candidates, all while scoring efficiency gains. Yet beneath this veneer of inclusion, the model quietly penalises career breaks—especially those taken for caregiving, illness, or age. No one intended discrimination; no one coded prejudice. Still, a generation of workers is invisibly demoted by mathematics that passes every test. These are not dystopian anecdotes. They are the quiet reality of modern automation: machines acting inside moral grey zones with superhuman speed and unexamined authority.

What unites these vignettes is not technology's failure, but our own impoverished definition of success. We have built systems that excel at optimisation but remain tone-deaf to context, intent, and human consequence. The paradox is elegant and devastating: the more competent the machine, the more dangerous its indifference. Compliance is not the same as conscience. What passes an audit may still violate our sense of justice, dignity, or care.

This book begins from a simple conviction: ethics cannot be patched onto machines after deployment. It must be designed in—engineered from the first line of the problem statement. Just as safety became a discipline in aviation and reliability in civil engineering, ethics must evolve from aspiration to infrastructure. We need to build systems where moral reasoning is not a policy footnote but an operational parameter.

The Age of Delegated Judgement

For millennia, humans reserved moral agency for themselves. We delegated labour to tools, but judgement remained a human monopoly. The loom never chose whose garments to weave; the press never decided whose words to print. Artificial intelligence shatters that boundary. Every day, systems decide who is creditworthy, who is employable, who is visible, and who is suspect. Our machines are no longer neutral instruments; they are decision-makers that interpret, sort, and rank human lives.

This shift is not just technical—it is civilisational. When we automate decision-making, we automate parts of justice itself. A recruitment engine that filters candidates performs a moral act: it allocates opportunity. A risk model that flags loan applicants wields power over livelihood. A recommendation system that shapes political discourse governs the visibility of truth. Yet we continue to speak of "bias mitigation" as though it were a mechanical defect, rather than an ethical negotiation.

Every age is defined by the moral questions it dares to mechanise. The Industrial Revolution mechanised labour and forced societies to invent rights for workers. The Information Age mechanised knowledge and birthed new notions of privacy and consent. The Age of Machine Judgement, which we now inhabit, demands nothing less than the mechanisation of ethics itself—or the humility to constrain our reach.

From Principles to Practice

In the past decade, organisations have published a flurry of "AI ethics principles". They extol fairness, transparency, and accountability in glossy decks and policy briefs. Yet, these virtues rarely reach the machine room. They remain abstract nouns, untethered from code, metrics, or incentives. The industry has learned to perform ethics without practising it. We have principles without procedures, committees without consequence, and compliance without conscience.

This book is written for those weary of moral theatre. It is for designers, engineers, policymakers, and executives who understand that real ethics begins not in manifestos but in specifications. The true site of moral failure in technology is not the line of code—it is the line of the problem statement.

When we mis-specify what the system is for, who it serves, and what harms it must avoid, we create errors that no later audit can repair.

Ethical engineering, then, begins with the problem definition. "The Problem Is the Specification," as the first chapter argues. To make fairness actionable, one must translate values into measurable constraints; to make safety testable, one must define red lines before a single model is trained. Throughout this book, we will move from slogans to scaffolding—from "be responsible" to "design responsibility into the workflow."

The Hidden Architecture of Choice

Every technology embeds a worldview. A map app presumes that time outweighs tranquillity; a social platform assumes that engagement equals value. These choices, trivialised as "user preferences", reveal a moral architecture as deliberate as any cathedral. Data is not neutral; it is the sediment of human decisions, each reflecting who was seen, heard, and counted. The world that machines learn from is a fossil record of our biases, omissions, and aspirations.

Yet the promise of AI lies precisely in its potential to transcend that inheritance—to help us imagine better worlds than the ones we trained it on. That ambition, however, requires humility about what machines can know and what they cannot. Chapter Four explores this tension: the ethics of not knowing. Uncertainty, far from being a flaw, is a moral signal—an invitation to pause, defer, or consult a human. In safety-critical systems, ignorance can be the most ethical output of all.

This book thus treats care, prudence, and doubt not as weaknesses but as design parameters. In the chapters that follow, "care" becomes a system property; "uncertainty" becomes a specification; "governance" becomes a form of engineering discipline. The ambition is to transform ethical reflection from a meeting agenda into a reproducible design practice.

The Human Frame

At the heart of this project lies an older question: what do we owe to one another, and to the users of our creations? Philosophers from Kant to Mill, from Aristotle to Rawls, have offered divergent answers—duties, outcomes, virtues, rights. This book does not ask the reader to choose a single doctrine. Instead, it seeks to operationalise pluralism: to embed multiple moral lenses within design itself. When duty clashes with outcome, or virtue with efficiency, the goal is not to eliminate the tension but to expose and govern it.

Chapter Two translates philosophy into product decisions. "Explainability as due process" reframes transparency as procedural justice, not public relations. "Dignity over optimisation" insists that humans are not behavioural variables to be nudged. In these pages, we move from moral theory to moral tooling, showing how to prototype respect, measure harm, and test fairness.

Culture as Code

No system is more ethical than the culture that builds it. Chapter Seven, "Culture: The Code You Don't See," explores how moral failure often begins not in algorithms but in meetings—those quiet rooms where deadlines erode principle and expedience passes for realism. It examines how language, incentives, and team composition silently shape moral outcomes. When dissent is punished as delay, ethics dies long before deployment.

To rebuild ethical capacity, we must re-engineer culture with the same precision we apply to systems. That means hiring for dissent, measuring what matters, and telling stories that dignify restraint. Culture, like software, is a living system. It can be debugged, versioned, and improved.

Governance with Teeth

Governance is often treated as bureaucracy's dull cousin: paperwork for those who missed the thrill of innovation. Yet true governance is the infrastructure of trust. Chapter Six, "Governance That Bites," defines a new grammar of accountability—risk registers, red-line logs, model cards, independent review boards. These are not shackles but supports: the scaffolding that allows innovation to rise without collapse. The goal is not to slow progress but to make it sustainable, credible, and lawful.

Crucially, governance is not the opposite of creativity; it is its condition. Just as a safety harness enables the builder to climb higher, robust oversight enables teams to take principled risks. The future of technology belongs to those who can innovate within constraints, not despite them.

The Ethics Engine

The final chapter turns philosophy into architecture. The "ethics engine" is not a metaphor but a modular framework—a set of technical and procedural components that translate moral principles into operational checks. It integrates value specifications into design pipelines, enforces harm constraints during deployment, and logs ethical trade-offs as systematically as performance metrics. In this vision, ethics is not an audit trail but a runtime feature.

An organisation equipped with such an engine does not rely on individual virtue alone; it builds morality into its systems of work. The shift is subtle but profound: from hoping people will "do the right thing" to ensuring the system makes the right thing easier to do.

A Moral Renaissance for the Machine Age

Every technological revolution forces a reckoning with what it means to be human. The loom unsettled labour; the printing press unsettled truth; the algorithm unsettles justice. Yet history suggests that progress endures only when it remembers its purpose. The machines we build today will inherit not only our data but our definitions of right and wrong. If we abdicate that task to convenience or compliance, we will automate our moral decline.

But there is another path: to build systems that extend our moral reach rather than erode it. This book invites you to that project—not as a technical manual, but as a moral companion. Together, we will examine how to specify values, test harms, and design with conscience. We will see how governance can have teeth, culture can cultivate courage, and uncertainty can dignify restraint.

The question that will guide every chapter is deceptively simple: when our machines act on our behalf, whose morality are they performing? The answer, inevitably, is ours. The only question that remains is whether we are willing to engineer it.

Chapter 1
The Problem Is the Specification

Every ethical failure in technology begins with a perfectly reasonable sentence. "We want to make hiring fairer." "We want to prioritise urgent cases." "We want to show people content they'll enjoy." Each sounds benign—admirable, even. Yet hidden within these phrases are choices so vast they can tilt lives. Fairer by what measure? Urgent to whom? Enjoyable at what cost? The trouble is not malice or neglect but mis-specification: the quiet translation of human ideals into mathematical objectives that mutate under optimisation. When fairness becomes a variable instead of a virtue, its meaning shrinks to whatever the model can measure.

Consider a credit scoring start-up that promises to democratise access to finance. Its engineers, earnest and well-intentioned, define success as "maximising repayment likelihood." The model performs beautifully—on paper. But soon, community lenders notice patterns: younger borrowers thrive while older ones vanish from approvals. The data reveals no explicit age variable, yet the proxy is clear—employment gaps, housing tenure, digital behaviour. The system is not ageist by design; it is ageist by proxy. In turning "fair lending" into a numeric target, the team redefined justice as convenience. The problem was never in the code; it was in the specification.

This chapter begins where most engineering handbooks end: with the problem statement itself. Before a single dataset is cleaned or a model tuned, ethical failure is already seeded in how we describe what the system is for. Specification is not an administrative step; it is a moral act. A misplaced word, a lazy metric, or an unspoken assumption can shape years of downstream harm. The task before us is to learn how to specify ethically—to translate values into variables without betraying their essence.

To do so, we must first acknowledge that ethics, like engineering, demands precision. Words such as *fair*, *safe*, or *inclusive* are invitations to ambiguity; they collapse under the pressure of optimisation. When a team debates fairness without measurement, the loudest voice wins. When they measure fairness poorly, the model wins instead. This book proposes a third way: to formalise values as measurable, testable, and reviewable artefacts that survive the velocity of product development. A value specification is a contract between aspiration and implementation. It defines not only what a system must achieve but what it must never do.

To make ethics executable, we convert ideals into *value specifications*—structured statements that translate moral goals into acceptance criteria. A specification might declare: "The system must not reduce approval rates for any demographic group by more than X% without justification." Behind that sentence lies a *harm table* mapping possible harms, affected stakeholders, and mitigation tests. Such tools shift ethical discourse from the abstract to the empirical. They let teams argue with evidence, not instinct. They also expose trade-offs that can be governed, audited, and revisited. This is ethics rendered in the grammar of engineering.

The need for such discipline becomes clear once we examine the three mis-specification traps that plague almost every AI system. The first is *proxy confusion*—mistaking what is measurable for what is meaningful. The second is *scope creep*—optimising beyond the system's legitimate remit, as when a health app becomes a surveillance tool. The third is *silent stakeholders*—those left out of design discussions yet left to bear the consequences. Each trap has a cost, but also a cure. Proxy audits expose hidden substitutions; remit charters define legitimate boundaries; stakeholder discovery surfaces the unseen. Together, they form a practical ethics toolkit: one that prevents crisis through disciplined foresight rather than post-mortem remorse.

These traps may sound technical, but their effects are deeply human. When a content-ranking algorithm mistakes outrage for engagement, it amplifies division. When a fraud detection model flags vulnerable claimants, it delays lifelines. Each instance reveals the same underlying pattern: a failure not of technology but of translation. The system did exactly what we told it to do; we simply told it the wrong thing. Ethics begins with telling machines the right thing, in terms they can compute without corrupting the value itself.

Accuracy—so often hailed as the holy grail of data science—illustrates this perfectly. Accuracy appears objective, apolitical, unimpeachable. Yet "average accuracy" hides moral asymmetry. A model that is 95% accurate overall may still fail catastrophically for the 5% least represented. In medical triage, those 5% may be patients whose conditions defy statistical generalisation; in fraud detection, they may be the most vulnerable claimants. Optimising for accuracy alone risks encoding injustice as efficiency. To correct this, we must move from single-metric triumphalism to *multi-objective ethics*—systems that balance predictive power against fairness budgets and harm constraints. The choice of threshold becomes a moral act; the act of abstaining, a sign of wisdom.

Consider the dilemma of an emergency response algorithm that predicts which ambulance calls are life-threatening. If it prioritises efficiency—responding fastest where it's most often right—it risks missing rare but fatal outliers. If it prioritises caution, it may overburden scarce resources. The moral frontier lies between these extremes, a Pareto surface of competing goods. Ethical design does not eliminate this tension; it maps it transparently. When teams report not just accuracy but *harm profiles*, they reclaim moral agency from the tyranny of the single number.

At the heart of ethical specification lies a paradox: we must constrain systems in order to make them safer, yet those constraints must evolve as context changes. To navigate this, we borrow a lesson from aviation and medicine—disciplines that learned to define what must *never* happen. A pilot has red lines; a surgeon has never events. In technology, these could be outcomes so unacceptable that no trade-off justifies them: "Never deny welfare benefits without a human appeal." "Never deploy a facial recognition model on minors." Such prohibitions are not expressions of fear but of clarity. They mark the perimeter of moral territory.

Writing the negative space—what the system must not do—brings moral rigour to ambiguous contexts. It transforms vague caution into enforceable policy. Red-line registers, escalation triggers, and accountable owners ensure that when pressure mounts, ethics does not evaporate into hand-wringing. The goal is not to eliminate human judgment but to support it under stress. When deadlines loom and dashboards flash, these guardrails preserve deliberation. They remind teams that morality is not a feature to be toggled, but a boundary to be respected.

If there is one habit that distinguishes ethical organisations from reckless ones, it is the *value pre-mortem*. Before a project begins, ask not what success looks like, but what failure would mean in human terms. Who might be harmed? Who might be ignored? What assumptions, if reversed, would break our claim to fairness? This simple inversion—imagining harm before heroism—saves millions in remediation and, more importantly, preserves trust. It is the cheapest, most powerful form of risk mitigation available, yet rarely practised.

Specification, then, is not the dry paperwork before the "real" work. It is the moral infrastructure on which the entire edifice rests. The art of specification is the art of ethics in code form. When we learn to express duties and rights as requirements, we convert philosophy into practice. A well-specified problem carries within it the blueprint of its conscience.

As you read this chapter, you will see how values become variables without losing their meaning; how teams can encode moral intention into measurable objectives; and how the discipline of specification can prevent the quiet tragedies of optimisation gone awry. We will move from conceptual clarity to operational precision, building the foundations of what this book calls the *Ethics Engine*.

Before we can build moral machines, we must learn to speak morality in a language machines understand. Specification is that language—an ethics of precision, written in code, tested in context, and lived through consequence. Everything that follows depends on getting this first step right.

From Values to Variables

In October 2019, the Dutch Ministry of Social Affairs suspended its welfare fraud detection system, known as SyRI, after the District Court of The Hague ruled it unlawful. The programme had analysed data from housing, tax, and employment records to flag citizens for potential fraud risk. Its designers insisted the algorithm was neutral—it simply correlated data points to detect anomalies. Yet it disproportionately targeted poorer districts and minority communities. When pressed, officials could not explain *why* certain people were flagged; the model's "success metric" had been defined as *fraud discovered per euro spent*. Fairness, privacy, and dignity had been lost between variables. The code was competent; the specification was not.

SyRI's downfall exposes the first and most pervasive truth in ethical engineering: the moral failure begins not in the model, but in the problem statement. Once fairness is translated into "fraud detection efficiency," justice is already a rounding error. Optimisation amplifies what we define, not what we intend. When we specify poorly, machines become mirrors for our vagueness. And because they operate with precision, they scale our mistakes with breathtaking efficiency.

The work of ethics in technology therefore begins at the same moment as engineering: the act of definition. To say *what a system is for* is to decide whose values will be encoded, whose harms will be tolerated, and whose voices will be silent. Yet most teams approach this step as a formality—a short paragraph on a ticket, a bullet point in a product brief. "Detect risk." "Optimise recommendations." "Improve retention." These phrases are not goals; they are ethical time bombs. A system optimising "retention" without constraint will inevitably learn manipulation. A model optimising "risk" will infer threat wherever powerlessness resides. The question is never whether a system has values—it always does. The question is whether we've specified them.

When engineers speak of "requirements," they mean testable outcomes: accuracy thresholds, latency budgets, throughput guarantees. When ethicists speak of "values," they mean justice, respect, autonomy, fairness. The bridge between these two worlds is the *value specification*—a structured statement that translates moral intention into operational terms. It treats rights and duties as acceptance criteria: obligations that must hold true for the product to be considered successful. This is not an act of moral decoration but of design discipline.

In 2020, Google's Responsible AI team introduced fairness constraints into YouTube's recommendation pipeline, specifying that recommendation exposure across demographic groups must remain within defined tolerance ranges. This constraint did not eliminate bias entirely, but it converted a philosophical aspiration—*equal opportunity to be seen*—into a measurable target. It changed what "success" meant to the algorithm. In that sense, the fairness constraint was not an afterthought; it was a design variable.

The act of specification is a moral geometry. It requires drawing boundaries where trade-offs will occur and documenting what must never be traded. A *harm table* makes this geometry visible: a grid that lists potential harms, affected stakeholders, and measurable indicators. For instance, a harm table for an automated hiring tool might include: "Disparate impact on candidates with career breaks," "False-negative rate for applicants with non-traditional education," "Denial of explanation or recourse." Each harm can be tied to a test case. A test that fails becomes a red flag, not an afterthought. In this way, ethical failure becomes a technical defect—fixable, discussable, reviewable.

But most organisations do not yet speak this language. They rely on intuition or debate: "Is this fair?" "Would we want this done to us?" Such conversations matter but collapse under time pressure. Product sprints reward the tangible. Ethics needs to be equally tangible: something that can be tested, not just felt. Templates for value specifications convert moral discourse into structured practice. A specification might read: "The system must achieve a recall rate above 0.8 for all protected groups, with variance not exceeding 0.05." Behind that crisp number lies a philosophical claim: *no group's dignity is expendable in pursuit of efficiency.*

This transition—from taste to test—is what makes ethics survive the sprint. Engineers do not ignore morality because they lack empathy; they ignore it because it lacks syntax. When fairness becomes a checklist item rather than a design constraint, it dies the slow death of good intentions. By contrast, a moral requirement encoded as a measurable parameter—one that blocks deployment when unmet—acquires force. It gains what engineers respect most: the power to fail a build.

Of course, not every value can be expressed numerically, nor should it. Some rights are categorical, not statistical. A facial recognition system may never store data on minors without consent, full stop. A predictive policing model may never be trained on ethnicity, regardless of correlation strength. These are *negative specifications*—ethical boundaries articulated as prohibitions. They coexist with quantitative goals, forming the perimeter of permissible design space. Together, they ensure that optimisation operates within a moral frame rather than beyond it.

There is precedent for this synthesis of ethics and engineering. In aviation, "never events" define unacceptable outcomes—loss of cabin pressure, mid-air collision, runway incursion. In medicine, the National Health Service classifies events that must *never* occur under any circumstances, such as surgery on the wrong body part. These prohibitions anchor decision-making when uncertainty and fatigue threaten judgment. Ethical engineering borrows the same logic. When a system's purpose is ambiguous, its red lines must be explicit.

To see how costly their absence can be, consider Facebook's News Feed redesign in 2018. Internal documents later revealed that the algorithm, optimised for "meaningful social interactions," amplified divisive content because outrage generated more engagement. The metric was mathematically sound but ethically hollow. Engagement is easy to count; social cohesion is not. A simple negative constraint—"do not reward interactions that increase civil toxicity beyond baseline"—might have prevented years of reputational and democratic damage. The machine was obedient; the specification was negligent.

Critics often object that value specifications risk over-formalising the inexpressible—that fairness, dignity, or respect cannot be reduced to metrics. They are partly right. Reduction is dangerous when it pretends to completeness. But absence is worse. The alternative to measurement is not moral purity; it is moral opacity. Without explicit constraints, power fills the void. Those with deadlines define fairness by expedience; those with profit motives define justice by retention rate. Measurement, however imperfect, makes values visible and therefore governable.

Still, a specification is only as sound as the process that produced it. Teams must identify whose perspectives shaped the definition, whose interests were marginalised, and whose harms were left invisible. The "silent stakeholder" problem haunts specification: those affected most are often consulted least. In the Netherlands, SyRI's targets were never shown the model's logic; in the United States, early credit algorithms ignored non-banking populations, treating the unbanked as untrustworthy by default. Both failures trace back to omission, not intention. The cure is *stakeholder discovery*: structured interviews, community testing, and participatory design that reintroduce the missing human data before the first line of code.

Specification is also temporal: it must evolve as systems encounter the world. A fairness threshold suitable at prototype may become unjust at scale. Continuous ethics testing—analogous to regression testing—ensures that yesterday's good does not become tomorrow's harm. In this sense, ethical engineering mirrors safety engineering: specification, verification, iteration. It is not a one-time moral declaration but an ongoing contract between system and society.

The deeper significance of specification lies in what it reveals about ourselves. To specify values is to make visible the hierarchy of goods we already act upon. When a company measures success in user minutes, it values attention; when it measures success in verified knowledge, it values truth. Specifications are moral x-rays. They expose our implicit theology—the gods our systems worship when no one is watching. To write them honestly is to confront the mirror.

If SyRI had been built with explicit value specifications, its downfall might have been averted. "The system must not disproportionately flag any postcode group by more than X% without cause." "All flagged cases must include explainable reasoning traceable to human review." Such sentences sound bureaucratic, but they anchor morality in infrastructure. They transform a political debate into a test suite. They would have forced the system's designers to measure harm before harm became policy.

The motif running through this subchapter—the bridge between intention and implementation—is the *translation problem*. Every ethical failure in machine design is a mistranslation. We intend fairness but specify efficiency; we intend inclusion but specify reach; we intend respect but specify compliance. The task is not to add ethics later but to speak it fluently at the point of definition.

As you continue through this chapter, keep one diagnostic question close: *If our system performs exactly as specified, will the world we produce resemble the world we meant to build?* That question is the first unit test of moral engineering. It is also the hardest to pass.

The Three Mis-Spec Traps

In March 2016, ProPublica published an investigation into a criminal risk assessment tool used in Broward County, Florida. The software, COMPAS—developed by Northpointe (now Equivant)—predicted the likelihood that defendants would reoffend. It was meant to aid judges in sentencing and parole decisions. When audited, the system appeared statistically sound overall. Yet the analysis revealed something disquieting: it was almost twice as likely to misclassify Black defendants as high risk and white defendants as low risk. Northpointe defended its model by citing accuracy parity. But accuracy was never the question. The value mis-specified was *justice,* translated into a proxy—recidivism prediction—divorced from the moral purpose it was meant to serve. The algorithm was optimising the wrong thing, perfectly.

This is the first trap: **proxy confusion**. When a value such as fairness, safety, or dignity is reduced to whatever can be measured, the measure becomes the master. The proxy displaces the principle. Every dataset contains surrogates that stand in for the unquantifiable—postcode for wealth, name for ethnicity, purchase history for trustworthiness. Over time, these stand-ins acquire moral authority, shaping decisions about employment, credit, and freedom itself. What was once a convenience becomes a creed.

Proxy confusion thrives because proxies are seductive: they offer clarity where ethics offers complexity. In digital advertising, "engagement" became the proxy for relevance. In 2018, Facebook's internal research (later revealed by The Wall Street Journal) showed that its engagement-driven ranking systems disproportionately amplified divisive and misleading content. Engineers had built precisely what they were asked to build: maximise engagement. Yet the real goal—informing and connecting people—was never specified in computable form. Engagement, measurable to the decimal, overwhelmed the intangible duty to inform responsibly. The tragedy was not technical failure but moral substitution.

Correcting proxy confusion demands a **proxy audit**: a systematic review of what each variable truly represents. A proxy audit asks uncomfortable questions—what human condition does this feature encode, and who pays when it misfires? In lending, for example, algorithms often use employment length or address stability as predictors of repayment. Both are proxies for socioeconomic privilege. When Apple and Goldman Sachs launched their joint credit card in 2019, female applicants reported receiving lower credit limits than their male partners despite identical financial profiles. Goldman's defence—that the algorithm never used gender—was precisely the problem. Gender had seeped in through proxies the designers never tested.

The corrective is neither sentimental nor purely technical. It is to trace the causal chain between data, proxy, and purpose, and to delete variables that act as moral ventriloquists. A well-run proxy audit functions like a mirror held to the system's assumptions: unflattering but vital.

If proxy confusion is the error of *mis-measurement,* the second trap—**scope creep**—is the error of *mis-intent*. It occurs when a system expands beyond its legitimate remit, smuggling in ambitions never consented to by those affected. What begins as a single-purpose model becomes an all-purpose judge.

The UK's "Prevent" strategy illustrates this vividly. Initially conceived in 2003 to identify early signs of radicalisation, it used behavioural indicators—attendance patterns, reading material, online activity—to flag individuals for further scrutiny. Over the following decade, its remit quietly widened to include "potential extremism" in non-criminal contexts. By 2015, teachers and healthcare workers were legally required to report "signs of vulnerability." The algorithmic systems built atop this framework extended the gaze even further, feeding data from education and health records into predictive policing pilots. Critics, including the UN Special Rapporteur (2017), warned that this expansion blurred the line between safeguarding and surveillance. The project had drifted from preventing terrorism to predicting deviance.

Scope creep is insidious because it disguises itself as efficiency. Once an infrastructure exists, it invites reuse. The logic is familiar: "We already collect the data—why not apply it here?" But every new purpose alters the moral contract. A model trained to allocate resources becomes a tool to enforce discipline. A recommender built to entertain becomes one to persuade. When boundaries dissolve, accountability evaporates.

The antidote is the **remit charter**—a document that defines not just what a system will do, but what it will *never* do. In 2021, the Ada Lovelace Institute proposed that AI projects include explicit "remit boundaries" reviewed by ethics boards before deployment. The idea is procedural yet profound: constrain ambition by design. In technical teams, a remit charter functions like an architectural blueprint; any new purpose requires a revision, not an assumption. Had such a charter governed the Prevent programme, its later expansions might have triggered formal review rather than bureaucratic drift.

The third mis-spec trap hides in plain sight: **silent stakeholders**. These are the individuals and communities who bear the consequences of design decisions but have no voice in defining them. Their absence from the specification phase ensures that their harms appear as "edge cases" later. The results are predictable: models that work well for the powerful and poorly for the marginalised.

A telling example emerged from Amazon's abandoned recruiting algorithm in 2018. Trained on ten years of historical hiring data, the model learned to downgrade CVs containing the word "women's"—as in "women's chess club captain." The system was never instructed to discriminate; it simply inferred that past hiring patterns were normative. The stakeholders most affected—women seeking technical roles—had no seat in the design or validation process. The silent became invisible.

Contrast this with the approach taken by the city of Helsinki in 2020, when it launched its open AI registry for municipal algorithms. Every system deployed by the city—from housing allocation to job matching—was published with an explanation of purpose, data sources, and affected stakeholders. Citizens were invited to challenge or refine these specifications before deployment. The policy slowed development but improved legitimacy. Participation, when institutionalised, turned silent stakeholders into co-authors of fairness.

The mechanism for this correction is **stakeholder discovery**—a structured process of identifying who the system touches and how. It borrows methods from ethnography and safety science: interviews, scenario testing, participatory workshops. The aim is not token consultation but epistemic expansion—to surface what the team does not know it does not know. When silent stakeholders speak early, they prevent the most expensive kind of failure: ethical crisis at scale.

The motif threading these traps together is *distance*. Proxy confusion creates distance between value and measure. Scope creep creates distance between purpose and practice. Silent stakeholders mark distance between decision and consequence. Ethical specification collapses these distances by reuniting designers with the human texture of their work.

Yet perfection is impossible. Not every proxy can be fully audited, nor every boundary fixed. There will always be ambiguity between intention and outcome. The discipline lies in recognising mis-specification not as a moral shame but as an engineering signal—a cue to revisit assumptions before harm compounds. This is where the **value pre-mortem** enters: a deliberate exercise in anticipating ethical failure before it manifests.

In a value pre-mortem, teams imagine their system has already caused harm and work backward to identify the mis-spec that made it possible. "Our loan algorithm was found discriminatory—how did our variable choice allow it?" "Our recommender radicalised users—what proxy stood in for engagement?" This rehearsal of regret transforms ethics from a post-mortem ritual into a design method. It costs little and saves much.

The cost curve of correction follows a familiar shape: a minor slope at concept stage, a cliff at deployment. Boeing learned this when software assumptions in its 737 MAX flight-control system—specifically the untested reliance on a single sensor—led to two crashes in 2018 and 2019. Each fix that could have cost thousands in design cost billions in crisis. The same pattern holds for moral design: the earlier the correction, the cheaper the salvation.

The three traps are not academic curiosities; they are patterns repeating across sectors. In lending, ad targeting, content ranking, and welfare, we see the same choreography of error: a proxy that distorts, a scope that swells, a stakeholder unheard. Their common origin is haste—the belief that ethics can wait until the system works. But systems *work* by definition; the question is what they work *toward*.

Every specification is a moral wager. To write one is to decide whose errors are tolerable, whose absence is acceptable, whose dignity is negotiable. Proxy audits, remit charters, and stakeholder discovery are not procedural niceties; they are the grammar of responsibility. They turn ethics from an aspiration into a series of verifiable commitments.

And yet, even with such tools, one question persists—the quiet motif that lingers at the end of every project meeting: *Who isn't in the room where this definition is written, and what will they pay for our precision?* Until that question becomes reflex, mis-specification will remain the cheapest mistake and the costliest lesson.

When Accuracy Harms

In 2019, a study by *Science* magazine uncovered that a healthcare algorithm used across major US hospitals—including by UnitedHealth Group—was quietly rationing care. The model, designed to predict which patients would benefit from extra medical support, had achieved an impressive overall accuracy score. Yet it was grievously wrong in one way: for patients with identical medical needs, Black patients were flagged for additional care nearly half as often as white patients. The system's creators had optimised for *cost of care*, assuming it mirrored health need. It didn't. Historical inequality meant Black patients incurred lower medical spending, not because they were healthier, but because they had been underserved. The model performed exactly as specified—and ethically, it failed completely.

This paradox—machines that are "accurate" yet unjust—defines one of the deepest fault lines in applied artificial intelligence. Average accuracy, that seductive single number, can conceal grotesque error patterns within subgroups. A classifier boasting 95% accuracy overall might still misclassify half the cases in one demographic. When base rates are skewed—say, when one group constitutes only a small fraction of the dataset—errors hide in the rounding. What looks efficient at scale becomes discriminatory in detail.

The moral danger of accuracy lies in its simplicity. It feels objective, universal, scientific. Yet accuracy is never a virtue in isolation; it is a lens, not a moral compass. A medical triage model that correctly predicts most mild cases but misses the gravely ill cannot claim ethical success. A fraud detection system that flags a small minority of vulnerable claimants to protect institutional budgets cannot claim neutrality. In each instance, the arithmetic of optimisation obscures the geometry of harm.

Take medical triage, where every percentage point of precision can mean a life saved—or lost. During the COVID-19 surge in Italy (March 2020), hospitals adopted algorithmic triage aids to allocate scarce ventilators. One such model, trialled in Lombardy, estimated survival probability based on age and comorbidities. Its aggregate accuracy reached 88%. But post-analysis by clinicians at the University of Milan revealed a grim distortion: survival predictions were consistently lower for disabled patients, whose chronic conditions inflated risk scores without corresponding reduction in survival chance. Accuracy, it turned out, was ethically brittle—reliable in aggregate, ruinous in edge cases.

In the financial domain, similar distortions arise through skewed *base rates*—the underlying frequency of an outcome. A 2020 audit of an Australian bank's fraud detection algorithm, reported by the Australian Human Rights Commission, found that migrant remittance accounts were 30% more likely to be falsely flagged as suspicious. The system had learned from historical data where fraud investigations were disproportionately targeted toward new immigrants. It achieved high "fraud detection accuracy" but only by perpetuating the investigative bias it inherited. Efficiency became discrimination by another name.

The corrective begins with recognising that **accuracy is plural**, not singular. A model's performance must be evaluated not as a single point, but as a vector of moral trade-offs—sensitivity versus specificity, group parity versus aggregate gain, precision versus dignity. In practice, this means constructing *multi-objective evaluations* that reveal the moral geometry hidden beneath the average. Engineers already plot *Pareto frontiers*—curves showing where improvement in one metric inevitably degrades another. Ethics demands the same literacy: to map where fairness and utility collide, and to decide transparently where the equilibrium should lie.

At Google Research, a 2021 fairness audit of its dermatology AI model illustrated this principle in action. The team discovered that the model, trained primarily on lighter skin tones, achieved 90% diagnostic accuracy overall but dropped to 66% on darker skin tones. The team rebalanced the training data and recalibrated thresholds per subgroup—a fairness budget of sorts—explicitly sacrificing a few points of global accuracy to reduce racial disparity. The revised model scored 85% overall but achieved parity across groups. The trade-off was deliberate, documented, and morally defensible. Here, *threshold choice* became an act of justice.

Thresholds, those apparently technical cut-offs where predictions turn into decisions, are moral hinge points. In fraud detection, for instance, a threshold that minimises false positives may leave genuine fraud unchecked, but one that maximises detection risks punishing the innocent. Each setting encodes a philosophy of risk distribution—who shoulders the burden of doubt. In welfare or healthcare, false negatives harm the vulnerable; in security or finance, false positives erode trust. To adjust a threshold is to draw a moral line through a probability curve.

Accuracy also misleads because it collapses harm into symmetry. In reality, errors are not equal. A false negative in cancer screening does not balance a false positive; a missed diagnosis costs a life, while a false alarm costs time. Ethical evaluation, therefore, requires *weighted harm functions* that reflect the asymmetry of consequences. In 2022, the UK's National Health Service began experimenting with such harm-weighted metrics for diagnostic algorithms, assigning different moral weights to types of error. These metrics moved evaluation closer to justice: not every mistake counts the same.

Yet metrics alone cannot absolve judgment. The pursuit of multi-objective optimisation reveals its own philosophical limits. Some values cannot be expressed in the same units. Fairness, dignity, and trust do not share a denominator with efficiency. That tension must be surfaced, not suppressed. A well-designed harm report—listing subgroup performance gaps, error asymmetries, and threshold rationales—acts as a moral ledger. It transforms invisible injustice into visible responsibility. When published, such reports also allow external scrutiny, turning accuracy from a claim into a conversation.

There is, however, a temptation to swing too far—to treat fairness adjustments as a purely technical fix. In 2018, the ride-hailing platform Uber introduced an algorithmic pay fairness adjustment to equalise driver earnings across geographies. It worked statistically but alienated drivers, who perceived the change as opaque and paternalistic. Accuracy and fairness were recalibrated, but *trust* collapsed. This counter-example underscores a crucial truth: moral performance cannot be detached from human perception. A fair model that feels unjust will fail socially, however elegant its metrics.

The motif that runs through these examples is *visibility*. Accuracy, as commonly reported, hides more than it reveals. Fairness budgets, harm reports, and Pareto frontiers turn accuracy inside out—they make visible the moral terrain beneath the metric. They allow decision-makers to see not just how well a model performs, but whom it serves and whom it neglects. The work is uncomfortable because it replaces triumphalism with trade-off. But trade-off, when named, is a form of accountability.

What makes this reframing urgent is not just the moral argument but the operational one. The cost of ignored subgroup harm compounds. In 2021, an AI-driven benefits system in the Netherlands was ruled discriminatory against low-income families, forcing the government to pay billions in restitution. The algorithm's overall accuracy had been impeccable; its injustice, catastrophic. Had harm reports and subgroup calibration been standard practice, the political fallout might have been avoided. Accuracy without ethics is fragility disguised as performance.

A counterpoint often raised is that multi-objective evaluation slows innovation. Teams, already under delivery pressure, cannot optimise for every metric simultaneously. This is partly true. But the answer is not to simplify morality; it is to prioritise transparently. Fairness budgets formalise moral trade-offs within resource constraints. They quantify what the organisation is willing to sacrifice in aggregate performance to reduce harm for a protected group. Explicit trade-offs prevent implicit bias. The discipline of setting a fairness budget is the opposite of paralysis—it is moral focus under constraint.

There is also a deeper epistemic lesson here. Statistical learning, by its nature, minimises *expected* error. Ethics, by contrast, demands attention to *who* bears that error. When we design systems to minimise global loss, we are also deciding which losses are acceptable. The mathematics of optimisation must be joined by the philosophy of distribution. To judge an algorithm's success solely by its accuracy is to mistake the mean for the moral.

When accuracy harms, it does so silently. The dashboards glow green, the metrics exceed targets, and yet trust corrodes beneath the numbers. The cure is not to abandon accuracy but to pluralise it—to replace the single figure with a frontier, the triumph with a tension. A truly ethical evaluation does not ask, *Is the model right?* It asks, *Right for whom, and at what cost?*

That question, posed early and often, transforms threshold setting from a calibration exercise into an act of care. It turns evaluation into ethics. And it leaves us, fittingly, with one test that no model can perform for us: when the graph looks good but the world feels wrong, will we have the courage to question the number?

Write the Negative Space

On 19 February 2003, Korean Air Flight 801 approached Guam in heavy rain. The autopilot disengaged moments too late, and the aircraft descended below glide path, striking a hill short of the runway. Two hundred and twenty-eight people died. Investigators later found that no mechanical fault caused the disaster; the crew had misread their altitude, and the airline's manuals lacked one decisive safeguard—a *never event* rule prohibiting descent below minimum altitude without runway contact. In the wake of the crash, aviation authorities across Asia formalised "red lines" for approach minima. They were blunt, enforceable, and transformative. The new discipline was born from tragedy: clear boundaries save lives when judgement falters.

The lesson extends far beyond the cockpit. Every complex system, from intensive care to credit scoring, contains moments where ambiguity kills—literally or metaphorically. Yet most organisations, especially in technology, prefer fluid principles over hard constraints. "Be ethical," "do no harm," "act responsibly"—noble phrases that evaporate under deadline pressure. What is missing is negative space: the explicit statement of what must *never* occur, the outcomes that no trade-off or efficiency gain can justify. Writing the negative space converts ethics from aspiration to architecture.

The term comes from art. In drawing, negative space is not emptiness but form by omission: the contour created by what is deliberately left blank. In moral engineering, the same logic applies. We define integrity not by everything a system can do, but by the boundaries we refuse to cross. Without such absences—without those white spaces of prohibition—ethical shape dissolves into good intentions.

Medicine learned this lesson painfully. The UK's National Health Service introduced its *Never Events Policy Framework* in 2009 after a decade of recurring surgical catastrophes: wrong-site operations, retained instruments, transfusion errors. Each event was entirely preventable and universally condemned. The solution was bureaucratically simple but ethically profound. By listing "never events" in a national register, the NHS converted moral taboos into enforceable obligations. A nurse no longer had to argue ethics mid-operation; the red line was institutional, not personal.

Between 2009 and 2019, incidence of wrong-site surgery dropped by more than half (NHS Improvement, 2020). Clarity, it turned out, is a form of compassion.

Technology rarely adopts this discipline. Software culture celebrates iteration, not prohibition. Teams pivot, patch, and A/B test, but seldom codify non-negotiables. Yet as systems gain agency, omission becomes danger. In 2018, a self-driving car tested by Uber in Tempe, Arizona, struck and killed a pedestrian. The internal safety review later revealed that the vehicle's software had been programmed to *ignore* certain obstacle classifications deemed "false positives"—for example, bags blowing across the road. The designers had never defined a red line for uncertain detections. The system had permission to doubt until it was too late.

Aviation and medicine treat "red lines" not as creativity's enemy but as its spine. Pilots train on checklists that blend procedural precision with ethical non-negotiables: never take off with unresolved safety alerts; never override a terrain warning. In hospitals, escalation triggers dictate when nurses must call senior clinicians, removing moral hesitation from life-or-death thresholds. These practices can inspire AI governance. An *escalation trigger* in algorithmic decision-making might require human review when confidence falls below a threshold, or when a model's prediction affects legal rights. A *never event* might forbid deploying an unexplainable system in a justice context, regardless of performance metrics.

The key innovation is not the list itself but the accountability it assigns. Each red line must have an *owner*: a person or team empowered to halt deployment without penalty. Ownership converts abstract prohibition into operational power. After the 737 MAX crises of 2018–19, Boeing revised its internal safety governance to designate explicit accountable engineers for each flight-control subsystem, reversing decades of diffused responsibility. Ethics without ownership, like safety without signatures, is theatre.

When technology firms attempt red-line policies, they often falter at the moment of enforcement. Google's 2018 internal rule prohibiting AI for weapons use—announced after employee protests—was clear in wording but opaque in scope. What counts as a weapon? Is surveillance infrastructure a weapon if used for targeting? Within a year, loopholes reappeared through contracts reclassified as "dual use." The lesson: red lines that cannot survive commercial reinterpretation are not boundaries but branding.

A *red-line register* addresses this drift. It functions as a living document—part specification, part moral logbook—listing forbidden actions, escalation criteria, and responsible signatories. Like an aircraft's minimum safe altitude chart, it codifies context: where are we allowed to go, and what happens if we stray? During emergencies, when ethical reasoning compresses under stress, the register speaks for the organisation's conscience. It protects careful thinking from the violence of urgency.

The metaphor of negative space also reminds us that clarity requires constraint. To draw a clean moral line, we must accept loss: of flexibility, of optionality, of speed. The tension between safety and innovation is not new. In 1979, after the Three Mile Island nuclear accident, the US Nuclear Regulatory Commission introduced the concept of *safety culture,* defining behaviours that must never be compromised. Critics warned that these constraints would slow energy progress; instead, they stabilised it. Reactors built under the new regime achieved higher reliability and lower incident rates. Constraints, properly designed, do not freeze progress—they permit it to endure.

But there are limits to codification. Too many red lines can paralyse. In emergency medicine, overzealous "never event" lists once led to excessive escalation, overwhelming consultants and delaying treatment. The NHS eventually refined its register to focus only on events that are *both preventable and catastrophic*. The same principle must guide digital ethics: red lines should be rare, public, and severe. A rule forbidding "harmful bias" is too vague; one forbidding *automated denial of essential benefits without human appeal* is enforceable. Precision distinguishes moral resolve from moral panic.

One counterpoint deserves attention: what if rigid rules prevent moral innovation? Could early red lines against certain technologies—facial recognition, predictive policing, behavioural nudging—stifle potentially beneficial forms? Possibly. Yet history suggests that prohibition often precedes progress. Early aviation bans on night flying, rescinded only after instrument navigation matured, forced engineers to invent safer tools. Temporary limits can cultivate capability. The moral question is not whether to forbid, but how to design red lines that evolve responsibly.

Writing the negative space also reshapes culture. It shifts ethics from personal virtue to collective discipline. When an engineer invokes a red line, they appeal not to conscience but to contract. The debate changes from "should we?" to "are we allowed to?"—a framing that transforms moral courage into procedural normalcy. The best cultures make ethical escalation as routine as bug reporting. In such environments, dissent is not defiance; it is maintenance.

A motif runs quietly through this approach: *clarity as care*. Ambiguity corrodes moral judgement by forcing individuals to improvise under pressure. Clarity—what we will not do—liberates thought for what we can do well. It is the ethical analogue of safety margins in design. When a bridge's load limit is declared, engineers can innovate confidently within it. When a machine-learning team defines its moral load limits—its red lines—it earns the same creative freedom.

Perhaps the most powerful aspect of negative space is its humility. It admits that no checklist can encode every virtue, that even the best teams err under pressure. Yet it also affirms that some harms are too grave, too irreversible, to risk. To name them is to respect the boundary between mastery and hubris.

The unfinished question remains: who should write these red lines—the engineers who understand the system, the ethicists who question it, or the public who endure it? Each claims legitimacy; none alone is sufficient. The answer will shape not just the future of technology, but the moral contour of the age. As with art, what we choose *not* to draw will define the image the world finally sees.

Chapter 2
What We Owe to Each Other (and to Users)

In August 2021, a man named Syed was denied unemployment benefits by a government algorithm in Michigan. The decision notice listed no human name, no reason, and no avenue for appeal. His payments vanished overnight. Months later, after a class-action lawsuit, the state conceded that 93% of these algorithmic fraud determinations had been false. The software had done what it was built to do—optimise for fraud detection—but no one had designed it to *explain itself,* or to *care* when it erred. Syed's case was not an accident; it was an ethical vacuum rendered in code.

Such moments force a question older than technology itself: what do we owe one another when we act through systems? For millennia, moral philosophy has wrestled with the tension between duty, outcome, and character. Yet in the age of algorithms, these theories no longer dwell in textbooks—they are compiled, deployed, and updated. A model that triages patients, curates news, or filters job candidates makes moral decisions with mathematical syntax. And its creators, whether they acknowledge it or not, inherit the weight of ethical choice.

The moral vocabulary of artificial intelligence is impoverished. "Fair," "safe," and "responsible" appear in policies, but few can say what those words mean operationally. When teams face real trade-offs—accuracy versus dignity, privacy versus utility—principles blur into expediency. This chapter argues for a repair: to rejoin philosophy with engineering, and to treat ethical reasoning not as corporate rhetoric but as *design logic*.

The task is practical, not abstract. Philosophical traditions, often dismissed as incompatible, become complementary lenses when translated into engineering form. *Deontology* asks whether duties are honoured—has consent been sought, bias tested, rights preserved? *Consequentialism* asks what outcomes the system creates—who benefits, who is burdened, who is left unseen? *Virtue ethics* asks what kind of organisation this design expresses—does it cultivate prudence, humility, or hubris? Each framework surfaces different blind spots; together, they form a moral triage that prevents tunnel vision.

In aviation safety, crews perform "duty checks," "outcome audits," and "character reviews" under different names. They ensure procedures are followed, consequences assessed, and culture examined. The same architecture can govern intelligent systems. Imagine a recommender model subjected to duty checks (no deception), outcome audits (balanced exposure), and character cues (does it cultivate addiction or agency?). This is not philosophy as ornament but philosophy as control loop.

The first section of this chapter, *Plural philosophies, practical choices*, introduces this translation. Readers will see how ethical doctrines become actionable artefacts—tables, tests, and triage sheets. Small case studies—autonomous vehicles, hiring tools, recommender systems—demonstrate the dangers of single-frame thinking. A team guided only by consequentialism may excuse manipulation as long as it "works." One bound to deontology alone may build systems too rigid to adapt. The craft lies in weaving the three together: duty defines the minimum, consequence tests the effect, and character sets the tone.

Yet philosophy without law is like code without runtime. The second section, *Rights, harms, and proportionality*, anchors moral reasoning in the legal principle of proportionality—a doctrine that spans European human rights law, data protection, and administrative justice. It asks three questions: is the action *necessary* to achieve a legitimate aim? Is it *suitable* for that purpose? And does it *minimally impair* rights? These are not legalisms but design tests. They turn vague discussions about "privacy trade-offs" into measurable questions of access scope, retention time, and data reach.

When an AI system processes medical records, proportionality decides whether it may access all records or only those strictly relevant. When it monitors employees for security breaches, proportionality governs not whether surveillance exists, but how intrusively it peers. Teams that learn to apply this principle create systems that are legally defensible and morally literate—respectful of rights without paralysing innovation.

The next thread—*Explainability as due process*—extends this logic from systems to citizens. Explanation is often treated as transparency, but its true purpose is *justice*. In legal systems, due process is the right to understand, contest, and appeal decisions that affect one's interests. The same procedural fairness must now migrate into algorithmic design. A model explanation that cannot be challenged is not an explanation; it is a monologue.

When Denmark's Employment Appeals Board introduced a human "second-look" review for AI-generated benefit denials in 2020, false rejections fell by 25%. Explanations changed outcomes because they reopened channels of accountability. In contrast, many private-sector explainability dashboards remain performative—confusing users with technical justifications rather than offering remedies. The future of explainability lies not in glossy visualisations but in procedural design: *decision receipts* that record reasoning, *contest channels* for appeal, and *escalation flows* that return moral agency to humans.

The final movement of this chapter, *Dignity over optimisation,* confronts the line between influence and coercion. As behavioural data becomes fuel for persuasion—nudging shoppers, steering voters, tutoring children—the difference between enablement and manipulation narrows. The moral test is no longer whether the product works, but whether it respects the autonomy of its user. Dignity, that stubbornly pre-digital virtue, must become measurable again.

The stakes are visible in education and health, where algorithms already shape life trajectories. Adaptive learning platforms that promise personalised instruction often end up streamlining curiosity into compliance, rewarding attention metrics over understanding. Fitness trackers that claim to "motivate" sometimes foster anxiety and dependence. These designs fail not because they miscalculate, but because they overreach—they treat humans as features to optimise, not as ends to respect.

To defend dignity, teams must introduce *guardrails for persuasion*. This means quantifying acceptable influence—testing how recommendation frequency, framing, or interface design affect user autonomy. It also means embedding *dignity thresholds* in evaluation pipelines: measurable points beyond which interaction becomes manipulation. These tools will not end ethical debate, but they will expose it to daylight, where decisions can be audited rather than improvised.

Across its sections, this chapter extends the central argument of *Ethics Engine*: that morality must be built in, not bolted on. We move from abstract virtue to executable constraint, from "what feels right" to "what passes test." Philosophy supplies the vocabulary, law provides the structure, and design operationalises both. Together they form a living ethics—tested like code, versioned like policy, and felt like conscience.

The motif that threads through all of this is *reciprocity*. What we owe to users mirrors what we owe to each other: explanation for decision, proportion for power, dignity for dependence. Systems inherit the moral character of their makers, and those makers are, in turn, shaped by the systems they build. To design justly is therefore to govern oneself as much as the machine.

The question that closes this introduction, and opens the chapter, is deceptively simple: if we delegate choice to algorithms, can we still claim to treat one another as moral equals? The answer, as the pages ahead suggest, depends on whether we remember that ethics is not what we *believe*—it is what we *build into the interface.*

Plural Philosophies, Practical Choices

In April 2016, *ProPublica* published an investigation into the COMPAS risk assessment algorithm used in Broward County, Florida. The system, designed to predict reoffending, claimed high overall accuracy. Yet when reporters analysed more than 7,000 cases, they found that Black defendants were almost twice as likely as white defendants to be falsely labelled "high risk." Northpointe, the company behind the software, defended its model: it treated all inputs equally, satisfied statistical parity, and met regulatory checks. By utilitarian metrics, it worked. By moral ones, it failed. The controversy split ethicists and engineers alike. Was the injustice in the numbers—or in the duties the designers had neglected to name?

Such conflicts expose a deeper problem: engineers tend to seek the single "correct" ethical framework when designing systems, while philosophy has long thrived on pluralism. Kant's deontology, Bentham's consequentialism, and

Aristotle's virtue ethics offer incompatible answers to what makes an action good. Yet in practice, each illuminates a different failure mode in technology. When algorithms violate duty, they dehumanise. When they fixate on outcomes, they justify harm. When they ignore character, they corrode trust. The craft of moral design lies not in choosing one lens but in combining them—creating an internal moral triage where duties, consequences, and virtues interrogate one another before code reaches production.

Deontology begins with the question of obligation. What do we owe, regardless of result? In data systems, this means honouring rights such as consent, privacy, and non-discrimination even when compliance slows delivery. A facial-recognition model that captures bystanders without permission may improve security, but it fails the duty test: it treats people as means, not ends. The General Data Protection Regulation (GDPR), enacted in 2018, operationalises deontological ethics at scale—requiring purpose limitation, data minimisation, and explicit consent. These are moral constraints expressed as law. They make duty executable.

Yet duty alone can blind design to consequence. In 2020, during the pandemic, several European health agencies initially refused to share anonymised mobility data with epidemiologists, citing privacy obligations. Weeks later, models predicting infection clusters faltered for lack of context. The result: delayed containment. A strictly deontological stance protected rights but failed lives. The moral lesson is technical as much as philosophical—duties must coexist with outcomes, or virtue collapses into rule-following without compassion.

Consequentialism, the ethics of results, asks whether a system's outcomes maximise benefit and minimise harm. This logic animates most AI metrics: precision, recall, impact, efficiency. It also explains why teams often rationalise bias as collateral damage in pursuit of scale. Facebook's 2018 feed-ranking overhaul, for example, optimised for "meaningful social interactions." The outcome: engagement rose, but polarisation intensified, as documented by the Wall Street Journal's internal leak in 2021. The algorithm succeeded by its own utility calculus while undermining the social good it professed to serve. Consequentialism without duty becomes exploitation disguised as optimisation.

Still, consequentialism's emphasis on feedback and iteration remains indispensable. It brings realism to moral design: systems must adapt to consequences, not just intentions. At the UK's National Health Service, the "Clinical Audit" tradition embodies this idea—regularly evaluating whether interventions achieve proportional benefit. Translating that to AI, an *outcome audit* might measure not only performance metrics but distributive impact: who gains, who bears risk, and whether harms are reversible. Consequentialism teaches that ethics, like engineering, must be empirical.

Then there is virtue ethics—the oldest and least mechanisable of the three. Aristotle's *Nicomachean Ethics* (4th century BCE) defines virtue as practical wisdom cultivated through habit. Applied to design, virtue ethics shifts focus from systems to their makers. It asks what kind of character the organisation exhibits in its defaults: humility before uncertainty, courage to dissent, temperance in ambition. When DeepMind's AlphaFold released its protein-structure predictions freely in 2021, many praised its generosity. Others noted it had learned from past criticism over data secrecy in healthcare partnerships. Whether deliberate or intuitive, that openness reflected a corporate virtue: stewardship over possession.

Virtue cannot be measured, but it can be signalled through rituals and roles. Review boards that welcome dissent, documentation that names uncertainty, and post-mortems that confess failure—all build moral muscle memory. Virtue ethics makes the invisible visible: culture as a system of guardrails. It is less about rules than reflexes—about engineers pausing before pushing code because they have been habituated to care.

Each framework corrects the excess of the others. Deontology prevents consequentialism from sacrificing the few for the many. Consequentialism prevents deontology from hardening into paralysis. Virtue ethics prevents both from degenerating into compliance theatre. The interplay is not theoretical; it is procedural. A moral triage can structure design reviews: *Duty check*—does this decision respect intrinsic rights? *Outcome audit*—does it improve collective welfare without unfair distribution? *Character cue*—does it reflect the kind of organisation we aspire to be?

Consider a product case. In 2021, a major online learning platform introduced an AI tutor that monitored student engagement. It raised alerts when users appeared distracted. Parents loved the data; educators recoiled. A duty check revealed privacy violations—the webcam data exceeded informed consent. An outcome audit showed gains in short-term performance but declines in student wellbeing. A character cue—what virtue does this promote?—exposed the design's paternalism. The triage did not yield easy answers, but it clarified trade-offs early enough to redesign.

A counterpoint often arises from practitioners: isn't philosophy too slow for agile cycles? The answer lies in translation. Philosophical reasoning can be re-expressed as worksheets and templates—artefacts that survive sprints. The "duty check" becomes a table mapping rights to test cases; the "outcome audit" aligns model metrics with harm scenarios; the "character cue" anchors design principles in behaviour. These tools move debate from taste to test, from posture to practice. When ethics lives inside the issue tracker, it starts to matter.

The motif threading through these approaches is *balance under tension*. Like a tripod, each leg stabilises the others. Remove one and the structure tilts—toward rigidity, opportunism, or vanity. Organisations that formalise only compliance (duty) breed bureaucracy; those obsessed with impact (outcome) drift toward moral hazard; those preaching culture (virtue) risk sentimentalism. True ethical maturity comes from accepting their friction as generative.

Still, pluralism carries risk. A company can cherry-pick frameworks to justify what it already wanted to do. The same virtue rhetoric that inspires one team can mask paternalism in another. Google's 2019 AI Principles, widely lauded for banning weapons applications, were later invoked to deflect criticism over surveillance partnerships. Plural ethics without accountability becomes moral relativism with better branding. The corrective lies in explicit triage: confronting conflicts rather than averaging them away.

Aviation offers a working analogy. Flight safety balances deontological rules (never fly below minima), consequentialist monitoring (fuel efficiency, route optimisation), and virtuous culture (captains who empower co-pilots to question). Each layer covers the others' blind spots. The same layered design can govern digital systems. A single moral lens invites catastrophe; redundancy saves lives.

Philosophy has always wrestled with scale—how to apply timeless principles to finite situations. Machine ethics inherits this struggle. A self-driving car approaching an unavoidable collision cannot consult Bentham, Kant, and Aristotle in sequence. But its creators can. They can encode duties (never violate explicit right of way), outcomes (minimise aggregate harm), and virtues (prioritise transparency over convenience). Moral triage becomes code architecture.

As we embed intelligence into infrastructure, the question is no longer whether machines can follow rules, but which rules—and whose character—they inherit. The ethics of AI will not be decided by manifestos but by spreadsheets, metrics, and meeting minutes. The frameworks of philosophy, stripped of ornament, must survive translation into process.

The unresolved tension remains: can plural ethics be systematised without being sanitised? Can we institutionalise moral diversity without dissolving moral courage? There will be no formulaic answer. But the discipline of asking—duty, outcome, character—before every major release is itself a moral act. It is philosophy rewritten as workflow, and perhaps the only kind that endures once the system goes live.

Rights, Harms, and Proportionality

In August 2020, the Court of Appeal in London ruled that South Wales Police's live facial recognition trials were unlawful. The case—*Bridges v South Wales Police*—turned not on whether the technology could identify faces, but on whether the force had narrowed its use to what was strictly justified. Who would be scanned? Where? For what purpose? The police had published policies, yet they had not constrained the system's reach with the precision that law demands. The court called it disproportionate. Five words, but a design brief in miniature.

Proportionality has become the hinge between legitimate innovation and unacceptable intrusion. Born in constitutional law and refined in human rights jurisprudence, it asks three questions that map cleanly to design: *necessity* (do you need this data or capability at all?), *suitability* (does it plausibly advance the stated aim?), and *minimal impairment* (does it restrict rights no more than required?). These steps are not rhetorical flourishes; they can be rendered as parameters, dashboards, and test cases. In a world of boundless capture and prediction, proportionality narrows the *aperture*: it decides how wide the lens may open before it floods the picture with collateral harm.

To see how, begin with necessity. Show: a healthcare insurer wishes to reduce hospital readmissions. Name: in 2019, a US system audited in *Science* was found to have used historical *spend* as a proxy for *need,* underserving Black patients because past spend reflected unequal access, not lower illness. Explain: necessity would have forced the team to prove that cost data were required to achieve the health aim, and to seek clinical indicators first. Implication: necessity cuts features that smuggle structural bias into the model, forcing a disciplined justification for every field in the schema. Design necessity is not a slogan; it is a feature whitelist that survives code review.

Suitability follows. Show: in 2014 at Luxembourg, the Court of Justice of the European Union annulled the Data Retention Directive in *Digital Rights Ireland*, holding that blanket retention of communications metadata was not sufficiently connected to combating serious crime. Name: the CJEU's judgment. Explain: suitability requires a plausible, evidence-backed link between the intrusion and the goal. If a programme stores *everyone's* data "just in case", the link is weak by design. Implication: engineers must articulate and measure a hypothesis of effect—if location logs are collected to detect benefit fraud, the team should predefine the pattern they seek, test its predictive value, and jettison the collection if the lift is trivial. Suitability turns "we might need it" into "we have shown it helps."

Minimal impairment sets the boundary for how much we may take. Show: Germany's Federal Constitutional Court has repeatedly cut back bulk data powers, insisting on targeted, graduated measures—tight source constraints, strict retention, layered warrants. Name: the Court's 2008 and 2010 judgments on telecommunications data retention and automated number plate recognition. Explain: even where the aim is compelling, designers must choose the least rights-restrictive path that still works. Does the model truly require raw voice data, or would hashed transcripts suffice? Do you need persistent identifiers, or could rotating tokens achieve the same linkage with less exposure? Implication: minimal impairment becomes a design principle you can verify—enforced sampling rates, ephemeral keys, local processing by default. It makes self-restraint measurable.

Comparative notes matter because teams operate across jurisdictions. The European proportionality test is explicit; Canada's *Oakes* test (1986) structures a similar inquiry; the UK's Human Rights Act imports Strasbourg's approach. The United States lacks a single proportionality doctrine in privacy law, but sectoral rules and Fourth Amendment "reasonableness" standards still reward necessity and narrow tailoring. Asia-Pacific models vary: Singapore's PDPA embraces "reasonable purposes"; Japan's APPI focuses on purpose specification and data minimisation. The message is practical: different legal grammars converge on the same engineering moves—limit scope, justify link, pick the least intrusive tool. A shared *floor* exists even when ceilings differ. If your architecture meets the strictest test you face, it will travel.

How do we transpose proportionality from counsel's memo to the build system? Treat each limb as a parameter. Necessity becomes an *access scope*: a table that lists every feature the model touches and the justification for inclusion. Suitability becomes an *effect size threshold*: a pre-declared minimum improvement required to retain a data source. Minimal impairment becomes a *privacy budget*: a cap on identifiability risk measured in concrete terms—retention days, re-identification probability, group exposure variance. These are not theoretical. They can block a pipeline when violated. They can be reviewed quarterly, like latency budgets or SLOs. When proportionality lives in code, it survives crunch time.

Consider a concrete product decision. A city transport authority proposes using passengers' phone MAC addresses to optimise station staffing. Necessity asks: can aggregate counts from Wi-Fi access points achieve the aim without device-level tracking? Suitability asks: does the model using MAC addresses actually outperform a model using simple turnstile entries in predicting staff demand? Minimal impairment asks: if device data are used, can we apply hashing with hourly rotation and delete raw logs within 24 hours? The answers are quantitative. They yield settings: sampling every three minutes, hashes that expire, retention capped at a day, model evaluation that compares effect sizes. The aperture narrows by design, not by afterthought.

A second example shows proportionality as a release gate. In August 2020, *Bridges* made British police reconsider facial recognition. A force now drafts a remit: cameras will run only at event perimeters where there is credible threat intelligence; the watchlist is restricted to individuals wanted for indictable offences; scans with confidence below a threshold trigger *no* action; logs of non-matches are never stored. These are design constraints born of the three-limb test. Later, an audit observes that the system still misidentifies women of colour at a higher rate. Minimal impairment requires either subgroup-specific thresholds, a higher global threshold, or suspension pending model retraining. Suitability demands proof that the intervention reduces crime *without* unacceptable false stops. Here, law writes the test plan.

A credible counter-example is the early public health response to COVID-19. In April 2020, several governments considered location-tracking apps to enforce quarantine. A strict necessity reading might have halted all digital monitoring. Yet some countries, including Germany, adopted the decentralised Apple-Google Exposure Notification system, designed to limit data collection while still serving the aim. The system did not track location; it used rotating Bluetooth identifiers stored locally. As evidence emerged, some jurisdictions adjusted retention windows and notification thresholds to minimise false alerts. Was large-scale digital exposure notification proportionate? Reasonable minds differed. But the design honoured the test: it tried to reduce impairment without destroying utility. The reconciliation is honest: proportionality is a discipline of *revision* as much as restraint. It learns.

Proportionality also governs model *reach*—where predictions are allowed to operate. A credit risk model might be accurate enough for loan pricing but too error-prone for fraud accusations with criminal referral. The same AUC does not justify the same domain. Treat reach as a switch, not a slope: even a high-performing classifier should be barred from contexts where false positives are irreparable. This is not Luddism; it is rights-weighted deployment. It respects that identical numbers mean different harms in different venues. The aperture changes with the scene.

Organisations resist proportionality because they fear paralysis. The remedy is to express safeguards as *design parameters,* not vetoes. Instead of saying "minimise data," say "no raw images persist beyond seven days; embeddings are salt-hashed; re-identification risk must remain below x% as measured by membership inference tests." Instead of "be transparent," say "generate a decision receipt with the features used, confidence interval, and escalation path within two seconds of adjudication." Instead of "limit scope," say "processing is confined to Table A; requests for Table B require an effect-size review and DPO sign-off." Precision frees movement. Teams can commit code against a clear yardstick rather than argue abstractions in Slack.

The same discipline hardens *justifications* to survive scrutiny. A privacy impact assessment should read like a lab notebook, not a press release. Identify the legitimate aim. Document why weaker means failed. Specify the measurable benefit sought. Fix a review date and success criteria. Record the alternatives you rejected and why. This is not performative compliance. It is memory. When challenged—by a regulator, a journalist, or your future self—you can show your workings. You can also reverse them when the world changes. Proportionality is a living proof, not a one-off certificate.

Culture carries the method. If product councils measure only adoption and revenue, proportionality will shrink to a legal checkbox. If they add *aperture metrics* to the dashboard—features per model, retention days per source, proportion of decisions with human appeal—then necessity, suitability, and minimal impairment become performance concerns. People ship what they measure. A quarterly "rights budget" review, where teams report reductions in access scope or retention without loss of utility, turns restraint into achievement. Celebrate the closed aperture that still delivers.

A final comparative note grounds ambition. The CJEU's *Schrems II* decision (July 2020) invalidated Privacy Shield transfers to the US on grounds that surveillance law there lacked proportionate limits. Some saw only trade friction. A better reading is architectural: if your system depends on cross-border transfers, build for demonstrable necessity and narrow access *before* legal winds shift. Canada's *Oakes* test likewise rewards time-bounded, evidence-backed intrusions with meaningful alternatives explored. These judgments are not mere paperwork; they are warnings that brittle architectures—those that rely on maximal capture—break under scrutiny. Design for the world as adjudicated, not only as engineered.

Proportionality can feel austere. It is. Yet its austerity protects the space where innovation earns trust. The method forces difficult substitutions. Sometimes the least intrusive means costs more. Sometimes it performs worse.

Sometimes it slows a sprint. But the alternative is a system that works until someone asks *why this data, why this reach, why this long?* and the room falls silent.

We return to the motif of the aperture. How wide should it be, and who decides? The next decision you take will answer both. Before you open the lens, ask three questions that no dashboard can dodge: do we *need* this data, does it *help,* and can we *take less* and still meet the aim? If the picture blurs as you narrow the frame, will you sharpen the model—or accept a blur to keep faith with rights?

Explainability as Due Process

In October 2022, a Dutch court in The Hague declared the government's SyRI welfare-fraud algorithm unlawful. The system—SyRI, or *System Risk Indication*—had flagged thousands of low-income households as potentially fraudulent, drawing on opaque data sources from housing, education, and taxation. Citizens could not see how they were scored, nor challenge the designation. The court's reasoning was surgical: the algorithm violated the right to a fair trial and respect for private life because it offered *no route to contestation*. What failed was not accuracy, but due process.

This ruling captured a turning point in the moral engineering of AI. For years, organisations equated explainability with *interpretability*—how clearly a developer could describe a model's internal mechanics. But interpretability, however elegant, means little to those on the receiving end of an algorithmic decision. A citizen denied benefits, a patient flagged high-risk, or a job applicant auto-rejected does not need gradient plots; they need recourse. The centre of gravity is shifting: explainability must serve the governed, not the builder. The ethical frontier lies not in better visualisations, but in systems that permit challenge, correction, and change.

To grasp this shift, recall the concept that guided centuries of administrative law: *due process*. It holds that power must explain itself before it acts, and must allow those affected to contest. In machine governance, this principle becomes the bridge between fairness as aspiration and fairness as operation. Transparency is no longer self-justifying; it earns legitimacy only when it alters outcomes.

Builder interpretability remains necessary but insufficient. In 2018, Google's DeepMind Health collaboration with the UK's Royal Free Hospital collapsed under scrutiny when regulators found patient data had been processed without a lawful basis. Internal interpretability was robust—engineers could explain every variable—but affected individuals could not access explanations or remedies. The case underscored the split between two moral layers: *epistemic* transparency (knowing how a system works) and *procedural* transparency (being able to contest what it does). Ethics demands both, but only the second confers dignity.

A working model of due-process explainability includes three interlocking artefacts: *decision receipts, contest channels,* and *second-look flows*. Decision receipts translate decisions into readable summaries: the inputs that mattered, the confidence interval, and the authority responsible. Contest channels offer structured routes to dispute—human-reviewed, time-bound, and logged. Second-look flows trigger escalation when thresholds are met: a disputed case, an outlier probability, or a harm report. Together, they transform an opaque output into a civic dialogue.

Take the Danish Employment Appeals Board, which in 2020 introduced a mandatory human review for any benefit denial produced by an algorithmic scoring tool. The intervention cut false rejections by a quarter and restored trust in the agency's digital systems. The mechanism was simple: the machine could recommend, not decide; every flagged case received a "second look" from a caseworker with authority to overturn. What mattered was not the explanation per se but the *right to rebuttal*. Fairness became procedural rather than cosmetic.

Contrast this with the United States' credit reporting regime. Consumers may obtain a "reason code" for adverse credit decisions, often a vague phrase such as "too many inquiries" or "insufficient credit history." While technically compliant with the Fair Credit Reporting Act, these codes rarely permit meaningful challenge. The result is a performative transparency—illumination without remedy. A code that cannot be acted upon is a story, not an explanation.

Explainability that changes outcomes must therefore close the loop. When an appeal is upheld, the correction should propagate back into model retraining, updating the system's assumptions. This is the moral equivalent of jurisprudence—cases that set precedents. The European Union's proposed AI Act hints at this logic, requiring not just documentation but mechanisms for "human oversight" and "post-deployment monitoring." Oversight without feedback, however, is supervision without learning.

An effective architecture for explainability-as-due-process also balances two temporal dimensions: *real-time transparency* (the decision receipt delivered at the moment of impact) and *systemic transparency* (aggregate reporting of appeals, reversals, and subgroup errors). The first grants fairness to individuals; the second sustains institutional accountability. The UK Information Commissioner's Office in its 2023 guidance suggested publishing "fairness dashboards" that track contest rates and reversals. The moral power of such dashboards lies not in numbers alone but in what they compel teams to fix.

A counterexample illustrates the danger of conflating clarity with justice. In 2021, a major U.S. healthcare algorithm known as Optum, used to prioritise patients for extra care, was made interpretable through feature importance graphs and SHAP values. The developers could show precisely which variables drove predictions. Yet analysis by Obermeyer *et al.* (2019) revealed that the model systematically underestimated risk for Black patients because it used historical healthcare costs as a proxy for need. The interpretability tools faithfully explained the *bias*.

They did not correct it. Due process would have required a patient-level challenge mechanism or a policy-level appeal to question the proxy itself. Interpretability made the failure visible; only remedy would have made it just.

The motif that threads this discussion is *voice*. Systems without channels for voice create moral silence, however technically sophisticated. Reinstating voice means accepting friction. Appeals delay closure, second looks cost money, audit logs invite scrutiny. Yet the alternative—silent automation—accumulates moral debt faster than technical debt. When reputational crises erupt, as they did with A-level grading in England (2020) or with content moderation errors across platforms, the damage stems less from error rates than from the absence of trusted appeal routes. Due process is expensive until you need it. Then it is the only thing that works.

To operationalise this discipline, organisations must embed contestability into their product lifecycles. A *decision receipt* should not be an afterthought; it should be part of the interface contract. Users should know who—or what—made a judgment, the main factors considered, and how to request a review. A *contest channel* should be tested like an API endpoint: does it function, and is it timely? The UK's Open Banking framework offers a precedent: consumers can challenge automated rejections through regulated dispute mechanisms. AI systems should aspire to the same procedural dignity.

Equally vital is the *second-look flow*—a structured escalation when the system itself expresses uncertainty or when human feedback flags harm. A fraud detection model, for instance, could trigger review for any case with a confidence score within a grey zone or when appeals surpass a defined threshold. This makes fairness auditable: teams can trace how many decisions crossed the second-look boundary and what proportion were reversed. When appeals reduce false positives or reputational exposure, due process ceases to be a cost centre; it becomes a risk control.

The benefits case is empirical. In 2022, a large European bank piloted an appeal mechanism for its mortgage approval model. Customers who disagreed with rejections could submit contextual data—job changes, savings history—reviewed by a small oversight team. The result: acceptance rates rose marginally, but complaint rates dropped by 40%, and no regulator intervened in the following audit cycle. The system became fairer and more defensible. Accountability, when routinised, pays dividends in resilience.

Sceptics argue that too much contestability paralyses automation. Yet due process does not mean every decision must be revisited; it means that *any* decision can be revisited with cause. The threshold can be calibrated: a triage that prioritises contested cases with significant material impact or statistical anomaly. This ensures human oversight is finite but meaningful. Law calls it proportional review;

design can call it escalation policy. Either way, the right to be heard becomes a feature, not a flaw.

Explainability-as-due-process also reframes fairness from a static property to a dynamic equilibrium. Every appeal, every reversal, every explanation that prompts change recalibrates the system toward justice. Fairness, under this lens, is not certified but maintained—like safety in aviation. A single incident may expose a latent defect; the value lies in the correction that follows. The appeal is not noise; it is feedback.

The unresolved question remains how far this procedural fairness can travel into machine learning models that are non-deterministic by design. If a large language model produces a decision-like output—such as summarising a medical report or recommending a sentence length—what does it mean to "appeal" its reasoning? One scenario is meta-explainability: building wrapper systems that store input-output pairs, enable human correction, and learn from contested examples. Another is normative pluralism: training models on diverse value frameworks so that their decisions can be compared, not just explained. Both ideas are nascent. Yet they suggest a path where explanation serves its ancient function—not to narrate, but to justify.

The motif of *voice* returns. A fair system listens as well as speaks. It gives reasons, but also revises them. As algorithmic governance extends into hiring, healthcare, credit, and policing, the critical test is no longer whether systems can explain themselves to engineers, but whether citizens can make those explanations *matter*.

So a question remains, one that should shadow every release review and ethics board: when your system explains itself, can the person on the other side do anything with that explanation? If not, the explanation is theatre. And justice, like trust, does not survive theatre for long.

Dignity over Optimisation

In 2018, a leaked internal report from Facebook revealed that its News Feed algorithms had systematically prioritised content eliciting "anger" reactions—because such posts drove higher engagement. The model optimised exactly what it was asked to: interaction. But the metric, efficient in isolation, became corrosive in aggregate. The resulting amplification of outrage eroded trust, polarised communities, and drew a Senate hearing within two years. The system had achieved its goal—and in doing so, humiliated its users. The scandal exposed a truth that ethics has long understood but engineers often forget: optimisation without dignity is manipulation by arithmetic.

Optimisation is the dominant grammar of machine intelligence. Every ranking, recommendation, and personalised feed is an optimisation problem, tuned to maximise click-through, retention, or conversion. Yet the human context of those optimisations is qualitative, not quantitative. There is a line between *enablement*—helping people achieve what they value—and *manipulation*—

nudging them toward what the system values. The difficulty lies in seeing where the gradient crosses that line. Dignity, the moral right not to be used as an instrument, becomes the missing constraint. To build it, we must learn to measure it.

The line is easiest to observe when it is crossed. In 2020, a University of California study found that algorithmic recommendations on YouTube were responsible for driving 70% of extremist video views. The recommendation engine's loss function rewarded watch time, not wellbeing. Suitability and necessity tests, as discussed earlier, might have reduced exposure, but dignity brings a deeper standard: consent to influence. Viewers did not knowingly agree to radicalisation as a side-effect of entertainment. The system violated their moral agency while technically performing perfectly. Dignity marks the point where persuasion turns into coercion through information asymmetry.

The challenge is that persuasion is not inherently unethical. Education, healthcare, and even public safety rely on it. The ethical difference lies in intent, transparency, and reversibility. When a system recommends a healthier meal plan or a language-learning streak, it can empower behaviour change if users understand the logic and can opt out. When it withholds clarity or exploits biases—variable rewards, loss aversion, social comparison—it trespasses on dignity. Optimisation is not neutral; it encodes the designer's theory of what counts as success.

Designers can express dignity as a measurable constraint. One approach is the *autonomy differential*: the gap between what a system knows about a user and what the user knows about the system's influence. The larger the gap, the higher the risk of manipulation. Netflix, for instance, in 2019 introduced an "explain your recommendation" feature, revealing key factors behind suggested content. That single interface shift reduced user suspicion and increased satisfaction. Transparency raised dignity because it narrowed the asymmetry. The metric could be formalised—tracking the proportion of influence channels made visible and reversible.

Education provides another concrete arena. Adaptive learning platforms like DreamBox or Coursera tailor pacing and content through reinforcement algorithms. When tuned responsibly, they sustain motivation without distorting agency. But when rewards are tied solely to time-on-task, they risk converting curiosity into compulsion. The ethical safeguard lies in proportionality and consent. Students should be able to understand the goal—mastery, not minutes—and calibrate their interaction accordingly. Some universities now publish "algorithmic syllabi," describing how recommendation systems operate. Dignity becomes operational when learners can say *no* without penalty.

Healthcare faces a parallel challenge. In 2022, the U.S. Food and Drug Administration reviewed digital therapeutics using gamified adherence strategies. One app for diabetes management offered escalating rewards for consistent tracking. Users reported improved compliance but also stress when missing entries triggered alerts. The design worked—but at a psychological cost. Respectful systems would replace punishment with reflection, prompting users to understand barriers rather than flagging failure. Dignity-sensitive optimisation treats data subjects as partners in reasoning, not targets of correction.

The motif of the *line*—the invisible threshold between enablement and manipulation—runs throughout this discussion. Every design team must decide where that line sits for their domain. Ranking systems for search results might prioritise relevance and diversity; social platforms might cap engagement-driven ranking beyond defined thresholds of emotional valence. These are not abstract ethics but policy parameters. In advertising, regulators already treat certain influences—targeting children, exploiting health fears—as violations of dignity. Technology can go further: dignity budgets could cap persuasive exposure per user, or models could report "persuasion intensity" alongside accuracy.

A counterpoint arises: what if persuasion serves a noble end? Public health campaigns, for instance, routinely employ behavioural nudges. The UK's Behavioural Insights Team has demonstrated that well-crafted prompts can increase organ donor registration or vaccination uptake. Yet even benevolent persuasion can slip into paternalism. The difference lies in *reversibility*. A dignified intervention allows the person to step back without penalty once informed. The moral test is procedural, not outcome-based: did the system respect the user's right to deliberate?

The tension between dignity and optimisation is, at heart, a question of *who decides the objective function*. If the objective is set solely by the provider—clicks, conversions, retention—users become inputs, not participants. If objectives are co-designed or multi-objective, dignity gains a foothold. In 2021, Mozilla experimented with "personalised metrics," letting users define their own optimisation goals for the browser's news feed: e.g., balance of topics, sentiment, or source diversity. Engagement dropped slightly; satisfaction rose sharply. The model respected the user's autonomy to decide what good looked like.

Dignity can also be tested empirically. One metric is *consent reversibility rate*—how easily and often users withdraw from an influence without friction. Another is *explanation uptake*—the proportion of users who can correctly describe why a recommendation appeared. A third is *agency retention*: whether users report feeling more capable after system use. These measurements translate dignity from virtue into variable. They let designers balance persuasion budgets the way they already balance latency or cost.

Of course, dignity has limits as a control principle. Some domains—like emergency response or cybersecurity—require decisive automation that precludes individual deliberation. There, the dignity constraint shifts from user to population: ensuring oversight, proportionality, and justification at the policy level. The moral actor becomes the institution, not the interface. The tension remains: speed versus self-respect. The reconciliation lies in context-aware governance rather than absolutism.

The economic argument for dignity is equally strong. Systems that manipulate users invite backlash, regulation, and attrition. In contrast, those that respect agency cultivate durable trust. Apple's privacy-centric design, often derided as "friction-heavy," has become a commercial advantage precisely because it signals respect. Ethical restraint, when engineered well, is not altruism but resilience. The algorithm that *can* stop itself earns loyalty.

The quiet motif returns: the line. It is easy to erase in the pursuit of metrics, yet every erased line invites revolt. The digital public has grown sensitive to when they are being gamed. The backlash against dark patterns, the popularity of screen-time tools, the rise of privacy-first products—all reveal a moral economy recalibrating toward dignity. Optimisation without constraint is no longer innovation; it is intrusion.

The unresolved tension remains vivid: can we quantify dignity without reducing it to another metric to optimise? Perhaps the safeguard lies in humility—the recognition that some values must be measured only to ensure they remain immeasurable in kind. The engineer's task is not to prove dignity, but to prevent its erosion by defaults that assume consent.

Before any ranking, recommendation, or persuasive model goes live, one question must be asked—not as philosophy but as a build condition: *Does this system respect a person's right to decide who they become?* If the answer hesitates, the optimisation is not ready.

Chapter 3
Data, Bias, and the Shape of the World

In 2016, a résumé-screening model built by Amazon was quietly decommissioned. It had learned to downgrade CVs containing the word "women's"—as in "women's chess club captain" or "women's coding society." The system had absorbed ten years of historical hiring data, a mirror polished by bias, reflecting the company's own past preferences back at itself. Engineers could not patch it. Every iteration rediscovered the same patterns, because the bias was not in the algorithm but in the world the data described. The model was not wrong; the world was.

That episode remains the most concise parable of modern artificial intelligence: the machine does not see people; it sees patterns of inclusion and omission. It learns from history, and history is not neutral. When we say that "data shapes the world," what we mean is that it reconstructs the contours of power, privilege, and visibility already etched into our institutions. Bias is not a bug. It is the statistical form of social inheritance. The question is not whether we can make data unbiased, but whether we can make its bias explicit, accountable, and correctable before it hardens into automated policy.

Every dataset is a worldview disguised as numbers. Who gets sampled, labelled, and measured decides who gets noticed and who disappears. Sampling frames act like camera lenses—some wide, some narrow, each distorting in a particular way. Label noise is the static of human judgement, where categories blur and misclassifications multiply. Yet within these imperfections lie the fingerprints of justice and injustice. If the lens is cracked, no amount of fine-tuning the learner can restore what it never saw. This is the first truth of data ethics: fixing fairness begins not in code but in collection. Sampling is destiny.

Consider how the world appears through the digital mirrors we build. Predictive policing maps crime to neighbourhoods already over-policed. Credit scoring models correlate creditworthiness with postcodes shaped by redlining. Content moderation systems flag dialects of African American English as toxic at double the rate of standard English, as shown in research by Sap et al. (2019). Each case reveals the same trap: the model performs well according to its metrics, yet performs harm in practice. The data were accurate to their sources, but their sources were unjust. The machine does not invent bias; it merely encodes our moral history with exquisite efficiency.

The chapter that follows unpacks four layers of that inheritance. It begins with the sampling problem—who gets seen and who is systematically excluded. Here we learn to draw *coverage maps*, to count not only what is present in the data but what is absent. Missingness becomes a signal. Subgroup performance sheets expose uneven accuracy; disparity becomes a design input. A case in hiring demonstrates how "experience gaps" masquerade as "merit," teaching teams to question metrics that reward privilege. The moral lesson is practical: you cannot fix bias downstream if it is upstream in the sample. Before adjusting algorithms, fix the lens.

From there, we turn to the politics of labels—the taxonomy through which systems make meaning. Categories are never neutral; they are acts of power. In medicine, diagnostic codes often flatten complex identities into single words, erasing cultural context. In online moderation, the line between hate speech and re-appropriation shifts daily. A slur in one community can be solidarity in another. When models inherit these contested categories, they perpetuate erasure. To mitigate, we move toward *hierarchical labels* that encode uncertainty and context, acknowledging what is unknowable rather than forcing brittle binaries. Good taxonomy is a civic act: communities must co-author the labels that define them.

Then comes bias mitigation—the technical heart of the chapter, but also its moral hinge. The industry's obsession with fairness toolkits has produced a cottage economy of metrics but little trust. Statistical parity, equalised odds, demographic parity—all elegant, all partial. This book takes a different path: instead of silver bullets, we build *portfolios* of mitigation, aligning each to product risk and accountability. Pre-processing fixes the data, in-processing constrains the model, post-processing adjusts the output. None are complete; each has costs. Case studies in lending and advertising show how to choose the right lever for the right harm. The goal is not perfection but *bounded imperfection*: a model whose errors are known, documented, and democratically chosen.

The final section of this chapter asks a question often avoided by technologists: *when should we not predict at all?* Some decisions—child protection, criminal sentencing, welfare allocation—carry irreparable stakes. The right to err safely is not evenly distributed; false positives in some domains devastate lives. Here, we formalise restraint as design: reversibility, appealability, and human oversight as conditions for automation. Predictive policing offers a cautionary tale: once prediction becomes policy, bias becomes law. The chapter proposes a *pause protocol*—a structured, independent review to decide when automation must yield to human judgement. Sometimes, ethics means stopping the build.

Threaded through all this is a simple motif: *data as lens*. The metaphor reminds us that bias is not a stain to scrub out but a distortion to calibrate. The same lens that can misrepresent can also reveal. A model trained on incomplete data teaches us where the world is incomplete. A misclassified image exposes the assumptions embedded in labelling. If we treat every dataset as a moral document—a record of who counts and who does not—we transform AI from an extractor of patterns into an instrument of reflection.

The stakes could not be higher. As AI systems decide who gets hired, insured, or investigated, bias migrates from the margins of academic concern to the centre of democratic life. The datasets that train these systems are the infrastructure of the future, yet most were never built for justice—they were built for convenience, speed, and scale. The task ahead is to rebuild that infrastructure with care: to write proportionality, inclusion, and humility into its scaffolding. Bias is not a technical debt; it is a civic one.

This chapter does not offer purity. It offers practice. It shows how to see the world not as data to be mined, but as meaning to be re-measured. It invites engineers, policymakers, and ethicists to ask not only *what works*, but *for whom*, *at what cost*, and *with what right*.

When you next confront a dataset—rows of numbers, tokens, or pixels—pause before optimising. Ask what the data believes about the world. Ask who wrote its assumptions, who was omitted, and who is defined by the labels. Then ask whether the prediction you plan to make should be made at all. The rest of this chapter is devoted to giving you the tools, and the courage, to answer.

Sampling Is Destiny

In 2018, Amazon abandoned an internal hiring algorithm after discovering it had systematically penalised CVs containing the word "women's." The model had been trained on a decade of past hiring data—tens of thousands of résumés, overwhelmingly from men. The system faithfully reproduced the company's historical behaviour, learning that male-dominated experience correlated with "merit." The engineers tried to remove gendered indicators, but the bias persisted. It hid in proxies—verbs, hobbies, and university names. No amount of model tuning fixed it, because the injustice was not in the code; it was in the sample. The dataset was a time capsule of an unequal world, and the algorithm simply read it fluently.

This episode remains the archetype of a deeper principle: sampling determines destiny. Before a single line of code is written, the moral geometry of a system is already drawn by the data it sees and, crucially, what it does not. Every dataset is a partial map of reality—cropped, filtered, and framed by the assumptions of those who built it. Sampling frames are moral artefacts. They decide which groups are visible, which outcomes are measurable, and which experiences vanish into statistical silence.

The bias introduced at this stage is not subtle; it is structural. In predictive policing systems, for instance, data drawn from historically over-policed neighbourhoods produce feedback loops of surveillance. The Chicago Police Department's "Strategic Subject List," discontinued in 2019 after public criticism, repeatedly flagged young Black men for "future crime risk," even when most had no criminal record. The model's accuracy appeared solid on paper—it matched historical arrest data—but its sampling frame had been warped by decades of discriminatory enforcement. The algorithm learned correlation, not culpability. Fixing such bias later through fairness metrics is like polishing a cracked lens: the image stays distorted.

The motif of the *lens* captures this moral geometry. Every model looks through a lens defined by its sampling frame.

A narrow lens magnifies the familiar but distorts the periphery; a wide lens captures diversity but at the cost of clarity. The task is not to find a perfect lens—none exists—but to understand its distortion and correct for it before the model learns from it.

To do that, practitioners are turning to *coverage maps*: visual audits of who and what a dataset actually represents. The Gender Shades project by Joy Buolamwini and Timnit Gebru (2018) exposed massive accuracy gaps in commercial facial recognition models. Accuracy for lighter-skinned men exceeded 99%; for darker-skinned women, it fell below 70%. The finding was not a flaw in the algorithmic architecture but a cartographic error in the data itself—datasets that overrepresented pale, male faces by orders of magnitude. Coverage maps made the absence visible. They became a diagnostic mirror, showing how the supposed universality of "AI vision" was built from a very narrow slice of humanity.

A complementary tool—*subgroup performance sheets*—extends that analysis. Instead of global accuracy, models are measured across demographic slices. Metrics are stratified: false positives for one group, false negatives for another. The imbalance becomes quantifiable, and therefore actionable. When the UK Home Office's 2020 passport-photo verification system was found to reject darker-skinned applicants more often, subgroup metrics revealed the disparity long before public scandal. The fix was not merely to re-train, but to expand the sample and redefine what "neutral lighting" meant in code. The algorithm was not racist by intention; it was colour-blind by design.

The hiring domain offers perhaps the clearest illustration of how sampling errors masquerade as objectivity. Recruitment datasets overwhelmingly reflect career continuity—linear, uninterrupted employment histories rewarded by corporate norms. Yet this definition of "experience" embeds structural exclusions: caregiving gaps, career switches, unpaid work. In 2021, a European HR analytics firm discovered that its model scored applicants with maternity breaks on average 30% lower than those without, even when controlling for qualifications. The explanation was banal but damning: the training set treated absence as disinterest. The data had equated privilege—the freedom to work continuously—with merit. Sampling had quietly rewritten social bias as statistical truth.

The corrective here is philosophical as much as technical. Teams must stop treating data as ground truth and start treating it as *partial witness*. Every dataset is a record of the conditions under which it was gathered: who had access, who trusted the process, who opted out, who was never asked. Sampling audits must therefore extend beyond numbers into context. When a dataset is built from public records, ask: who is less likely to appear in public records? When it relies on voluntary surveys, ask: who has reason to mistrust institutions? Sampling bias is often the shadow of historical harm.

Yet even the most conscientious teams face a dilemma. Correcting for underrepresentation through *re-weighting* or *oversampling* can reduce bias on one axis while increasing it on another. Balancing gender may worsen class imbalance; balancing ethnicity may distort regional distribution. The trade-off is unavoidable because fairness is multi-dimensional and resources finite. The solution is not to chase a perfectly balanced dataset—an illusion—but to document where imbalance remains and why it was accepted. Ethical documentation converts impossibility into accountability.

Label noise compounds the problem. Every data point carries not only a feature but an interpretation—a label assigned by humans under pressure, with limited knowledge. In content moderation datasets, for example, annotators decide what counts as hate speech, humour, or protest. Their judgements are coloured by culture and context. A 2020 study by the University of Washington showed that African American English was mislabelled as offensive at nearly twice the rate of Standard American English. The labels taught the model to inherit linguistic prejudice. Noise, in this sense, is not random; it is patterned along social lines.

When labels distort meaning, fairness metrics become meaningless. The remedy lies in *label audits*: cross-checking annotation consistency across diverse groups, introducing uncertainty scores where consensus fails, and incorporating hierarchical categories instead of binary ones. The goal is epistemic humility—recognising when data cannot bear the moral weight placed upon it. Some teams now append "label confidence" fields to training records, allowing models to learn uncertainty rather than false certainty. A humble model may perform worse on benchmarks but better on justice.

The counter-example often cited is medical imaging. Here, large, well-sampled datasets have delivered genuine performance gains across diverse populations. The UK's NHS DeepBreath project (2021) demonstrated lung-cancer detection models trained on mixed demographic data with minimal disparity in outcomes. The controlled conditions and objective labels—radiologist-verified diagnoses—reduced social bias. Yet even this apparent success reveals a hidden asymmetry: the data came from patients already within the healthcare system, excluding those most underserved. The model generalised well within its own context but could not correct systemic inequalities in access to care. It was fair only within a boundary.

This limitation underscores the central motif: the lens cannot correct what lies beyond its frame. Engineers often reach for technical fixes—debiasing algorithms, reweighting schemes—but these only refine the pixels inside the picture. They do not expand the picture itself. The more radical act is to re-sample reality—to collect new data that represent the missing, the marginal, the misclassified. In practice, that means engaging communities, adjusting consent processes, and funding representation as infrastructure. Bias begins in data budgets, not in model architectures.

Fixing the lens before fixing the learner demands institutional discipline. Teams should maintain *sampling charters* that declare their frame: what populations the dataset covers, what it excludes, what trade-offs were made. These charters act like ethical metadata—statements of scope and limitation. They turn sampling from a silent assumption into a visible commitment. When things go wrong, the charter becomes an accountability map, showing where and why the lens was narrow.

The unresolved tension, however, remains: how wide should the lens be before the system collapses under its own complexity? Broader samples improve fairness but degrade specificity; tighter samples improve accuracy but entrench exclusion. Each project must choose where to stand on that continuum, knowing that neutrality is a myth.

Perhaps the ultimate question is this: when the dataset reflects the world as it is, should the goal be to model it faithfully or to model it better? Every choice—what to sample, what to label, what to ignore—is a moral act disguised as technical design. Sampling, then, is not just the start of the pipeline. It is the first draft of justice.

Labels as Politics

In 2019, researchers at the University of Maryland examined Facebook's automated moderation logs and discovered something disquieting: posts reclaiming the word *queer*—

used by LGBTQ+ users as self-affirmation—were being flagged as hate speech. The same classifier that failed to detect genuine harassment treated reclaimed identity language as inherently toxic. The model was not malicious. It was obedient. It learned its categories from human-labelled data in which annotators, following corporate guidelines, had tagged the term as slur rather than solidarity. A single taxonomic decision erased an entire community's right to self-definition.

That quiet misclassification reveals a truth engineers often forget: categories are arguments frozen into code. Every label reflects a worldview, a boundary between what counts and what does not. The politics of naming is ancient—think of Linnaeus's 18th-century species classifications or the racial typologies of colonial anthropology—but machine learning has made it automatic, invisible, and global. Once encoded, these categories travel at the speed of infrastructure, determining whose words are suppressed, whose symptoms are recognised, whose existence is legible to systems that claim to be neutral.

The motif of *buckets*—the crude containers into which data are poured—captures the danger. Labels are buckets, and the world rarely fits cleanly inside them. Moderation algorithms sort speech into "acceptable" and "unacceptable," medical classifiers label bodies as "normal" or "disordered," hiring models mark applicants as "fit" or "unfit." Each bucket simplifies complexity into decision. The moral problem is not that simplification occurs—it must—but that the criteria for simplification are rarely revisited once deployed. Buckets ossify. Politics becomes geometry.

Take health coding. In 2022, the World Health Organization's ICD-11 classification officially redefined "gender incongruence" from a mental disorder to a condition related to sexual health. That single shift, achieved after years of advocacy, changed access to care and insurance for millions worldwide. Before that, under ICD-10, transgender identities were clinically pathologised. The category itself produced harm: patients avoided treatment to escape stigma, and insurers refused coverage for procedures deemed "elective." The label was not descriptive; it was prescriptive—it told institutions how to behave. Taxonomy shaped reality.

Digital health systems inherited those codes wholesale. Machine-learning tools built to predict hospital admissions or triage risk used diagnostic codes as features. Thus, outdated or biased categories propagated through clinical AI. A study in *Science* (Obermeyer et al., 2019) found that a widely used U.S. healthcare algorithm underestimated the medical needs of Black patients by 50% because it used historical healthcare spending as a proxy for health status. Black patients had historically lower spending due to unequal access, so the model read under-treatment as low risk. The label "healthy" became a statistical fiction with life-and-death consequences.

The counter-argument is that classification is indispensable. Without categories, systems cannot scale. Spam filters, triage models, and translation engines rely on discrete classes to make decisions. Ambiguity stalls automation. But this is precisely the moral frontier: to design categories that preserve ambiguity where necessary rather than erase it for convenience. Hierarchical labels with uncertainty capture are one way forward. Instead of forcing a tweet to be "hate" or "not hate," a model can assign a probability distribution and flag uncertainty for human review. In medicine, hierarchical taxonomies allow symptoms to live under multiple provisional diagnoses until evidence stabilises. Systems that can say *I'm not sure* harm less.

Building such nuance requires rethinking governance. At present, taxonomies are treated as frozen assets—defined by experts, shipped in datasets, rarely revisited. A more ethical practice is *taxonomy governance*: explicit, participatory processes that treat labelling as an evolving dialogue. Wikipedia, for all its flaws, demonstrates this principle in miniature. Its categories are debated, documented, and version-controlled; every edit has a talk page. Machine-learning taxonomies should aspire to the same openness. Communities most affected by classification—patients, users, creators—should participate in revision cycles, bringing lived experience into the ontology.

Moderation again offers a cautionary and instructive case. In 2021, TikTok admitted to suppressing content from creators with disabilities and LGBTQ+ identities, ostensibly to "protect" them from bullying. The result was a form of algorithmic paternalism—silencing in the name of safety. The moderation categories that triggered suppression were drawn from a risk taxonomy built without community input. When activist groups challenged the policy, the company introduced a "creator council" to review enforcement categories. The revision didn't solve bias, but it introduced feedback—a rudimentary form of democratic taxonomy. Systems that evolve through critique do less harm than those that equate authority with accuracy.

Label noise adds another layer of distortion. Human annotators, often underpaid and overworked, bring cultural context to their task whether they mean to or not. When asked to label "toxic" comments, annotators' own sensitivities and norms shape the dataset. Researchers at Jigsaw (2020) showed that annotator demographics significantly affect toxicity ratings; comments deemed acceptable by one cultural group were flagged as offensive by another. Instead of averaging these differences away, we can encode them—using multi-perspective labelling that captures dissent as data. Diversity of annotation becomes a statistical expression of pluralism rather than an obstacle to consistency.

The motif of the bucket returns: some overflow, others remain empty. Hierarchical and uncertain labelling turns the rigid bucket into a network of smaller vessels—connected, permeable, revisable. In practice, this means allowing labels to coexist across layers: a tweet might be "humour" under one schema and "political commentary" under another. A medical note might carry both "anxiety" and "grief" as co-diagnoses with uncertainty scores. By allowing overlap, systems acknowledge that lived experience rarely conforms to single categories.

A credible counter-example is the financial domain, where categories are tightly regulated for consistency. Credit scoring systems cannot accommodate ambiguity; a loan is either approved or denied. Here, probabilistic labels may be impractical. Yet even in these high-stakes contexts, governance can introduce transparency about the assumptions behind labels—what constitutes "default," how "risk" is defined, whose data anchor the baseline. The constraint does not excuse opacity. It demands compensatory explanation.

The ethical test for any taxonomy is not whether it classifies accurately, but whether it classifies *justly*. Accuracy measures internal consistency; justice measures external consequence. When classification systems harm, they do so not only through mislabelling but through erasure—forcing people to choose between boxes that don't fit or being excluded entirely. Consider ethnicity categories in national censuses. The UK Office for National Statistics revised its census categories in 2021 to include "Roma" as a distinct ethnic group after advocacy revealed systemic undercounting. The addition was statistical, yet its moral effect was representational: the group became visible in data, and thus in policy.

Visibility, however, brings new risks. When categories become legible to power, they can also become targets. The same datasets that empower can expose. After the Rwandan genocide, national ID cards listing ethnic categories—Hutu and Tutsi—became instruments of death. This historical shadow haunts every act of labelling. To make a category is to make a claim about identity that can be weaponised. The lesson is sobering: even well-intentioned classification can be perilous when governance lags ethics.

In the practice of building AI, taxonomy is destiny disguised as metadata. The schema behind a dataset decides which differences matter and which dissolve. Yet most teams treat the schema as inherited infrastructure, not moral design. The path forward is to elevate taxonomy governance to first-class practice—drafted with domain experts, community representatives, and continuous revision. Versioned ontologies, audit trails for label changes, and uncertainty thresholds for contested terms should be treated as hygiene, not heroics.

The unresolved tension endures: if categories are necessary for order but dangerous when rigid, how do we balance legibility with freedom? Systems too flexible lose utility; systems too fixed lose humanity. Perhaps the answer is procedural rather than technical—to make the *process* of naming as transparent, plural, and accountable as possible.

Every label should come with a provenance: who defined it, when, for what purpose, and how it might evolve.

Before a dataset becomes a model, and a model becomes a policy, one question must be asked—not of accuracy, but of authorship: *who has the right to name whom?* The integrity of every intelligent system begins there.

Bias Mitigation That Actually Works

In 2021, the U.S. Consumer Financial Protection Bureau fined Trustmark National Bank $5 million for discriminatory mortgage practices. The bank's credit-scoring model had systematically under-approved Black and Hispanic applicants across Memphis and Jackson, even when income and debt levels were equivalent. The model's architecture was not exotic—logistic regression, weighted features, decades of lending data. The harm lay in its training history: it learned to mirror past approvals, not equal opportunity. When regulators demanded corrective measures, engineers faced a dilemma still unresolved across industries—where exactly to intervene. Should they adjust the data, the objective, or the outputs? Their choice determined not just the model's fairness but its legality.

This is the heart of bias mitigation as engineering ethics: deciding where to place the scalpel. Pre-processing, in-processing, and post-processing are not rival techniques but moral positions, each redistributing accountability between data, model, and decision-maker. The right choice depends on the harm, the context, and the capacity for oversight. The myth of a single fairness fix—a silver bullet—is what keeps bias remediation performative. The practice that works builds portfolios: layered, auditable mitigations tied to evidence and ownership.

The motif of *surgery* fits well. Bias mitigation is not cosmetic—it is triage. You identify where the wound originates, decide how deep to cut, and measure what recovery means. Some wounds are superficial; others lie beneath the skin of the data itself.

Pre-processing operates upstream, before the model ever trains. It targets the composition and structure of the dataset. The classic example is reweighting: assigning higher importance to underrepresented groups so their influence on the model increases. In 2019, IBM Research's "AI Fairness 360" toolkit popularised such methods, combining reweighting with *disparate impact removal*—a statistical technique to equalise feature distributions across protected attributes. The advantage is simplicity: once debiased, the same data can feed multiple models. But the limitation is fragility. Reweighting can distort natural relationships, making the model behave erratically when deployed on unbalanced real-world data. Like a bandage applied too tightly, it can restrict circulation.

The more ambitious pre-processing approach is *resampling*, replacing or synthetically generating examples from underrepresented groups. In credit scoring, this has been used to augment low-income applicants' data. Yet it introduces an epistemic hazard: synthetic data reflect the modeller's imagination, not lived reality. The German fintech N26 explored this method in 2020 for loan risk prediction but halted trials after auditors found that synthetic data inflated default risk for minorities—a textbook example of bias correction creating new bias. The implication is clear: you cannot fake fairness into existence; it must be grounded in real, measured diversity.

In-processing takes a different stance: it embeds fairness into the learning objective itself. This approach modifies the loss function so the model is penalised for unfair outcomes. Google's "Equality of Opportunity in Supervised Learning" paper (Hardt et al., 2016) remains foundational here, proposing fairness constraints during training to equalise false-positive and false-negative rates between groups. The advantage is mathematical precision; the drawback is interpretability. Adding fairness penalties can obscure causal structure, producing models that satisfy fairness metrics while degrading overall reliability.

One striking example arose in online advertising. In 2019, Facebook (now Meta) adjusted its ad delivery algorithm to comply with U.S. anti-discrimination laws after investigations showed that housing and job ads were being microtargeted along racial and gender lines. Engineers embedded fairness constraints directly into the optimisation layer. While this reduced bias in aggregate, advertisers complained that cost efficiency dropped by 20%. The fairness-adjusted system made equitable exposure expensive. The ethical question shifted from *whether* to be fair to *who pays* for fairness.

Post-processing lies downstream, intervening after the model outputs its predictions. This is often the most feasible path for organisations with legacy systems. Threshold adjustment—altering decision cut-offs by demographic group—can align outcomes without retraining. For example, in 2020, the UK's Office for National Statistics piloted a post-processing calibration method for its labour market classifier to reduce gender disparities in occupational coding. The technique achieved statistical parity but raised controversy: critics argued that differential thresholds violated equal treatment. Fairness gained, legitimacy lost. This illustrates the paradox of post-processing—it can fix symptoms but rarely the disease.

To move beyond isolated fixes, teams increasingly employ *bias portfolios*: coordinated combinations of pre-, in-, and post-processing techniques, each governed by evidence. A financial institution might begin with reweighted sampling (pre), add fairness-regularised loss terms (in), and calibrate thresholds by validation feedback (post). Each layer mitigates the others' weaknesses. Portfolios work because they mirror how bias originates—in layers, not in silos.

Ownership, however, is the missing pillar. Fairness fails when responsibility diffuses. A bias mitigation decision tree helps map accountability to action. It begins with diagnostics: where does the disparity emerge—data distribution, model behaviour, or decision rule? From there, ownership follows logically. Data teams own pre-processing; model developers own in-processing; product managers own post-processing. Each must provide evidence—statistical tests, audit trails, documentation—showing why their chosen intervention is proportional to the harm. This evidence culture converts fairness from aspiration into auditability.

A telling case comes from Apple Card in 2019, jointly managed with Goldman Sachs. Users, including prominent technologist David Heinemeier Hansson, reported that women received substantially lower credit limits than men with identical financial profiles. Goldman's engineers insisted their model was "gender-blind." Regulators later concluded that the bias arose not from overt discrimination but from feature correlation—variables such as income history and credit age indirectly encoded gendered inequality. The fix required not a new model but a new *governance workflow*: a fairness review step in model approval, independent of developers. The lesson: bias mitigation without governance is self-deception.

There is a temptation to treat fairness metrics—statistical parity, equal opportunity, predictive equality—as interchangeable moral currencies. They are not. Each encodes a different ethical stance. Equal opportunity prioritises parity of error; demographic parity prioritises parity of outcome. Choosing between them is choosing between values: equity versus equality, risk versus reward. Bias mitigation that works begins with this moral acknowledgement. Technical decisions are value judgements in disguise.

Counter-examples illuminate the limits. In fraud detection, pre-processing that balances minority groups may increase false negatives, letting real fraud slip through. Regulators will not accept ethical justification for systemic risk. Likewise, in medical triage, post-processing by demographic group may violate clinical impartiality. The reconciliation is procedural: involve domain experts early, document trade-offs, and make deviations from fairness metrics explicit rather than covert. Transparency does not eliminate bias, but it redistributes trust.

The motif of *surgery* returns. Every intervention leaves a scar. Bias mitigation is not about erasing bias—it is about managing its harm through controlled incisions. Just as surgeons document complications, machine learning teams must document residual bias: what remains unmitigated, why, and how it will be monitored. Continuous evaluation—bias regression testing—turns fairness from a one-time repair into ongoing maintenance.

A credible benchmark for this practice is the Dutch Central Bank's 2022 "AI Fairness Audit Protocol." It mandated independent fairness reviews for high-impact models, requiring quantitative tests, stakeholder consultation, and revalidation cycles. Instead of mandating specific techniques, it required *proof of proportionality*: that the chosen mitigation matched the nature and magnitude of the harm. This proportional model could define the next decade of AI regulation. It rewards good judgement over mere compliance.

The unresolved tension remains philosophical. Bias can be reduced but not removed; fairness can be measured but never finalised. Each intervention reflects a trade-off between moral clarity and operational reality. The future of responsible AI depends less on inventing new algorithms and more on institutionalising judgement—teaching teams to ask not "Which technique performs best?" but "Which combination aligns with our duty, evidence, and accountability?"

The measure of bias mitigation that truly works is simple yet profound: not how fair the model becomes in isolation, but how fair the organisation becomes because of the model's reflection. Fairness is not an artefact of code. It is a habit of governance.

When Not to Predict

In 2016, the Chicago Police Department launched an algorithmic system to forecast who might commit a violent crime. The "Strategic Subject List," developed with the Illinois Institute of Technology, analysed arrest records, social networks, and demographic variables to identify individuals most at risk. At its peak, the system contained over 398,000 names. The model's creators called it predictive policing; critics called it pre-crime. By 2019, the programme was shut down after an internal audit revealed that it had failed to reduce violence and had disproportionately targeted young Black men. It had made thousands of predictions about who might harm or be harmed, yet none of those predictions could ever be meaningfully confirmed or contested. It treated probability as guilt and risk as destiny.

This case illustrates a foundational limit of prediction: not every future worth anticipating is worth automating. In some domains—law enforcement, child protection, welfare eligibility—the act of predicting alters the reality it observes. A forecast can trigger surveillance, intervention, or stigma that transforms the very lives it claims to merely model. When predictive systems cross from inference to intrusion, restraint becomes the highest form of intelligence.

The motif of the *red line*—a deliberate boundary drawn to preserve dignity and rights—anchors this section. Knowing when not to predict is as vital as knowing how. Prediction, by design, reduces uncertainty. Ethics, by necessity, lives with it.

The principle of reversibility offers one diagnostic test: can a prediction, once made, be undone? In finance, algorithmic risk scores can be revised, appealed, and recalculated. In contrast, in child protection or criminal justice, predictions attach to names, not numbers. When the Dutch child welfare authorities deployed the *SyRI* system in 2018—a risk-scoring tool to detect welfare fraud—it combined housing, employment, and tax data to flag "high-risk" families. Thousands of households in Rotterdam were stigmatised without explanation. In 2020, a Dutch court ruled SyRI unlawful, citing violations of privacy and human rights. The decision's core reasoning was reversibility: there was no way for citizens to know, challenge, or correct their digital profiles. Once the prediction was made, it stuck.

Reversibility and appealability should define the "do-not-automate" list—the inventory of decisions too consequential, too irreversible, or too morally ambiguous to outsource. Predictive policing and child welfare screening both fail this test because their outcomes embed into social institutions that rarely forget. By contrast, predictive maintenance in aviation or logistics involves reversible stakes; a faulty forecast may cost money, not liberty. The distinction is moral, not technical: where automation magnifies asymmetry between system and subject, restraint must prevail.

The *pause protocol*—a structured mechanism to suspend or escalate deployment—is an emerging governance tool for this restraint. Before a predictive model is launched, teams conduct reversibility and harm audits. If outcomes are non-reversible or appeal channels absent, deployment pauses pending review. This concept borrows from medicine, where "never events" and "go/no-go" criteria prevent irreversible harm. The idea is procedural humility: an institution admits that some actions are too entangled with human judgment to be delegated.

Child protection illustrates this vividly. In 2020, the state of Oregon halted its predictive risk model for child abuse investigations after public backlash. The system had been designed to prioritise limited social-worker resources by predicting which families were most likely to reoffend. But the data used—poverty indicators, prior interactions with welfare services—made disadvantage itself a proxy for danger. Parents already under scrutiny were re-flagged, reinforcing bias. The prediction became a self-fulfilling prophecy. The state's chief data officer, Gretchen Kafoury, acknowledged that despite technical accuracy, the model failed a deeper test: moral recoverability. Once a family was labelled "high risk," their relationship with the state was permanently altered.

A credible counterpoint is healthcare triage. Predictive systems there routinely prioritise patients based on likely outcomes—life expectancy, treatment success, resource scarcity. These predictions also carry grave stakes, yet they are reversible and contestable: clinicians can override algorithms, patients can seek second opinions, and models are retrained on evolving evidence. The safeguard is procedural redundancy—humans remain in the loop with authority, not as ornamentation. The same cannot be said of many public-sector prediction systems, where human oversight often means rubber-stamping machine output.

The tension is not between automation and empathy but between speed and due process. Predictive policing promises efficiency—intervene before crime occurs—but collapses when confronted with rights that require due procedure. In 2017, the UK's Durham Constabulary piloted the Harm Assessment Risk Tool (HART), predicting reoffending likelihood using local custody data. The tool achieved respectable accuracy on paper—around 62% according to internal validation—but no clear mechanism existed for appeal or redress. Once categorised as "high risk," individuals faced stricter bail conditions. The prediction quietly replaced deliberation with classification.

The implication extends beyond policing. Any predictive model embedded in public administration—be it for housing allocation, immigration screening, or social benefits—requires an *appealability clause*. This is not merely legal formality; it is an ethical circuit breaker. Without it, errors persist unchallenged and become institutional truth.

To institutionalise restraint, some jurisdictions have begun drafting "do-not-automate" registers. The Canadian Directive on Automated Decision-Making (2019) mandates that federal agencies assess algorithmic impact and prohibits full automation for decisions affecting rights or safety without explicit ministerial authorisation. The policy introduces proportionality: the higher the risk, the greater the required human oversight. Such frameworks operationalise what philosophers have long argued—that justice is not merely about correct outcomes but about the *right to contest* them.

The counter-example is the commercial sector, where predictive advertising thrives precisely because outcomes are reversible. A mis-targeted ad wastes a click, not a life. Yet the same techniques, when applied to political persuasion, can manipulate civic will. Cambridge

Analytica's operations during the 2016 U.S. election demonstrated how predictive profiling—trained on millions of harvested Facebook records—could shape individual voter behaviour without their awareness. While each micro-persuasion was reversible in theory, the cumulative effect was not: it altered democratic conditions. The boundary between persuasion and coercion eroded silently. The question becomes: how reversible is influence itself?

This brings us to the motif of the *red line*. Institutions must articulate, in advance, where prediction ends and human judgment resumes. The red line is not static; it shifts with context and evidence. In public safety, a red line might prohibit predicting individual guilt. In healthcare, it might prohibit predictive triage without consent. In finance, it could forbid credit scoring that lacks explainability or appeal. Drawing these lines transforms ethics from rhetoric into infrastructure.

Independent review is the final safeguard. A model that cannot withstand external scrutiny should not govern human futures. After the failure of Chicago's predictive policing programme, the city's Office of Inspector General established an independent oversight mechanism for all subsequent analytic projects. External auditors now assess fairness, transparency, and proportionality before deployment. This shift from secrecy to scrutiny reframes accountability as a precondition of legitimacy. Prediction becomes a privilege, not a presumption.

Yet a deeper paradox remains. Prediction, by its nature, aspires to eliminate uncertainty. Human rights, by contrast, depend on it—the right to be presumed innocent, the right to be judged as an individual, not a probability. The more we automate foresight, the less room remains for forgiveness.

The enduring question for every designer, policymaker, and engineer, then, is deceptively simple: *Can this prediction be undone?* If the answer is no, the system belongs on the pause list, not in production. Some parts of the future demand not prediction but patience. The measure of moral maturity in machine intelligence may lie not in how much it can foresee, but in how wisely it chooses to refrain.

Chapter 4
Causality, Uncertainty, and the Ethics of Not Knowing

In the spring of 2018, a Chicago high school implemented an algorithmic discipline tracker designed to predict which students might become "disruptive" during the term. It drew on attendance logs, grade histories, and disciplinary reports from previous years. Within weeks, teachers noticed a pattern: students from the same postcodes—largely working-class Black neighbourhoods—were repeatedly flagged as "high risk," even when their records were clean. The system was correlating absence with defiance, late buses with moral failing. The students had not changed; the lens had. What the algorithm mistook for causation was context. And yet, its labels became prophecy—detentions increased, opportunities narrowed. The model's creators called it proactive discipline. Parents called it prejudice by proxy.

The moral hazard of correlation lies precisely there. When data predict without understanding, the innocent are punished for their proximity to the guilty, and interventions lose their humanity. The challenge is not that algorithms err—they always will—but that they err *consistently*, encoding ignorance as authority. To build ethical intelligence, one must teach machines to know what they do not know. That requires causality, humility, and a new moral grammar for uncertainty.

Causality, at its simplest, asks "why," not just "what." It distinguishes between smoke and fire, between signal and stereotype. A credit-scoring model that penalises applicants from low-income postcodes, for instance, confuses correlation for cause—it assumes that geography drives default rather than structural inequality. Causal diagrams and minimal graphs, borrowed from econometrics and epidemiology, help separate genuine drivers from stigmatic markers. They are moral instruments disguised as mathematical ones, guiding interventions towards repair rather than sorting. Ethics, in this light, becomes fidelity to inference—the courage to demand that explanations reflect reality, not convenience.

The motif of the *lens* threads through this chapter: each predictive model is a lens shaped by its maker's beliefs, its data's shadows, and its capacity to admit doubt. A clear lens reveals; a warped one blinds. And yet, even the clearest lens cannot eliminate uncertainty. It must be calibrated, not worshipped.

The first part of this chapter, *Correlation's Moral Hazard*, examines how well-intentioned models reproduce injustice when they mistake proximity for causation. We revisit domains where data's logic turns punitive—credit, hiring, school discipline—and see how causal inference techniques can act as moral correctives. The goal is not omniscience but clarity: fixing the lens before fixing the learner.

From there, we move to *Counterfactual Fairness*, a notion that blends philosophy with formal modelling. It asks a provocative question: would a decision have changed if the individual's protected attribute—gender, race, disability—were different in a counterfactual world? If yes, the system is biased. This approach, elegant yet fragile, demands honesty about its assumptions. In health insurance, for instance, counterfactual fairness could correct for genetic predispositions that are beyond human control—but it could also erase legitimate group differences that reflect biology, not bias. The power and peril of counterfactuals lie in their seduction: they offer fairness through hypotheticals, yet the moral weight rests in what is left unmodelled. Transparency, not perfection, must be the standard.

Uncertainty then takes centre stage. Overconfidence in models—whether of risk, disease, or behaviour—is an ethical failure, not a technical one. Overstated certainty breeds complacency; understated doubt erodes trust. Calibration, abstention, and defer-to-human mechanisms are the new safeguards. A model that can say *I don't know* is not weak; it is civilised. In emergency response systems, for example, selective prediction—where an algorithm declines to forecast when confidence falls below a threshold—has been shown to reduce false alarms and improve trust among dispatchers. Interfaces that communicate uncertainty with dignity, not defensiveness, turn ignorance into a feature of moral design.

And then comes the hardest lesson: the cost of false hope. Predictive systems often err asymmetrically—the harm of a false positive differs profoundly from that of a false negative. In welfare or benefits fraud detection, flagging an innocent claimant can destroy a livelihood; missing a fraudster costs money. Which error matters more? The answer depends not on mathematics but on values. By quantifying those asymmetries—through participatory threshold setting and decision curves—we can make ethics empirical. Communities, not corporations, decide what trade-offs they are willing to bear. The shape of these moral curves becomes a democratic expression of risk tolerance and empathy.

Across these sections runs a unifying premise: that ethics in artificial intelligence is not only about what we know, but about how we handle what we *cannot*. The pursuit of certainty, long glorified as progress, now reveals its shadow. Systems that claim to predict everything risk destroying the moral space for forgiveness, learning, and surprise. There is virtue in ambiguity when lives and rights are at stake.

Causality, uncertainty, and restraint thus form a triad of ethical intelligence. Causality demands we see clearly; uncertainty reminds us we see partially; restraint ensures we act proportionally. Together they reframe what it means to "know" responsibly in the age of data.

The stakes could not be higher. In courts and clinics, classrooms and credit bureaus, models increasingly mediate trust. A misplaced correlation can cost a future; an unacknowledged uncertainty can cost a life. To build moral machines, we must re-teach them what human reason once held sacred: that knowledge is not the same as understanding, and that wisdom begins at the edge of what we cannot know.

As you read ahead, keep one question in view—the lens's question: when a machine predicts, does it illuminate truth, or merely amplify our blindness? The answer may define not only the future of ethics in artificial intelligence, but the meaning of intelligence itself.

Correlation's Moral Hazard

In 2019, the U.S. Consumer Financial Protection Bureau (CFPB) released its findings on credit scoring disparities. The report confirmed what many had long suspected: applicants from majority-Black neighbourhoods were being denied loans at nearly double the rate of their white counterparts, even when income, employment, and debt ratios were equivalent. The culprit was not overt prejudice but correlation. Credit models had treated postal codes, payment histories, and utility data as objective indicators of creditworthiness. Yet these variables, forged in decades of housing segregation and unequal infrastructure, carried the residues of structural disadvantage. A postcode became a proxy for poverty, and poverty a proxy for risk. The system punished the blameless—not through malice, but through mathematics.

This is correlation's moral hazard: the ease with which patterns mistaken for causes translate into punishment. When algorithms infer behaviour from proximity, they transform context into guilt. The hazard is not simply technical—it is epistemic and moral. It arises when we confuse what predicts with what explains, when a variable's usefulness to the model eclipses its justice to the human.

To navigate this hazard, causal reasoning re-enters as the discipline's conscience. Correlation says "these things co-occur"; causality asks "why." That single shift—asking *why* instead of merely *what*—changes not only the quality of our predictions but the fairness of our actions. Causal diagrams, often referred to as Directed Acyclic Graphs (DAGs), now serve as ethical cartography for data systems. They map relationships between factors, distinguishing the true drivers from stigmatic markers. This act of mapping is not sterile modelling—it is moral engineering. A line wrongly drawn can condemn thousands to unjust classification.

Consider the credit case again. If income instability leads both to missed payments and to residence in high-turnover areas, then postcode is not the cause but a symptom. A model that penalises postcode mistakes symptom for source. By explicitly representing these relationships in a causal graph, we can identify which variables are spurious correlates and which reflect genuine drivers of repayment. Interventions then shift from exclusion (rejecting applicants) to repair (supporting income stability). Causality transforms punishment into problem-solving.

The same distortion occurs in school discipline. In 2018, the Los Angeles Unified School District (LAUSD) introduced a data-driven system to flag students at risk of suspension.

Variables included attendance, previous disciplinary incidents, and even lateness patterns. Within a semester, Black students—already 8% of the district population but 25% of suspensions—were flagged at rates 3.5 times higher than white students. Post-analysis revealed that one of the strongest predictors in the model was *teacher referral history*. In practice, that meant the model learned from existing bias: teachers who disproportionately referred minority students for discipline created a feedback loop of algorithmic punishment.

The district's eventual correction—a causal analysis conducted with UCLA's Civil Rights Project—demonstrated how variable disentanglement could expose injustice. Once the team mapped the causal graph, it became clear that "lateness" and "teacher referral" were not independent causes but downstream effects of transport access and differential scrutiny. By removing them as causal inputs and replacing them with direct, objective measures of behaviour, the false positives halved. Causal reasoning did what rhetoric could not: it made fairness operational.

Minimal graphs—those stripped to the smallest set of necessary causal links—play a crucial role here. They enforce parsimony, forcing designers to justify every connection they assert between data and outcome. Each line must represent an empirically or theoretically defensible mechanism, not a convenience. The moral virtue of minimal graphs lies in their discipline: they make unjustifiable inference visibly uncomfortable. In credit, in hiring, in discipline, the fewer the lines, the clearer the accountability.

But even causal reasoning has its limits. Consider predictive health analytics. A 2020 study by Obermeyer et al., published in *Science,* revealed that a widely used U.S. hospital algorithm assigned Black patients lower risk scores than white patients with the same disease severity. The model used *healthcare cost* as a proxy for *health need,* assuming higher expenditure implied worse illness. In reality, structural under-treatment of Black patients meant lower recorded costs—thus lower risk scores. Causal diagrams could have exposed this false proxy by showing that "cost" was not caused by "need" but by "access." Yet causal correction alone cannot fix the deeper inequity: even perfect modelling cannot substitute for justice in the world the data reflect.

That is the counter-example's lesson: causal clarity cannot redeem causal cruelty. We may know precisely why inequality appears, but knowing is not the same as changing. Ethics begins where accuracy ends—when we ask what to *do* with the knowledge.

A visible motif emerges across these domains: the mirror. Every model holds a mirror to the world that made its data. If the reflection is distorted, we must decide whether to polish the glass or change the room. Most organisations polish the glass—tweaking models, adding fairness constraints—without confronting the underlying asymmetries. Yet the mirror, when used honestly, is diagnostic. It shows the gap between correlation's comfort and causality's challenge.

This distinction carries profound implications for intervention design. Correlational models optimise for sorting—ranking individuals by predicted risk or value. Causal models, by contrast, enable *intervention testing*: they simulate what would happen if we acted differently. In educational policy, this difference is decisive. When the U.K. Department for Education reviewed its exclusion algorithms in 2021, causal analysis revealed that improving school transport reliability had a stronger causal impact on attendance than punitive truancy fines. Sorting answers "who"; causality answers "what helps." Ethics, therefore, is not measured by equal outputs but by faithful inference—the integrity of cause and effect.

The moral hazard of correlation deepens when systems scale. Large platforms, especially in hiring and credit, deploy opaque correlation matrices at continental scale. In 2020, Amazon discontinued its AI recruiting tool after discovering gender bias: the model downgraded résumés containing the word "women's," as in "women's chess club captain." It had learned this from historical hiring data, which reflected past male dominance. A causal diagram could have made this bias visible, separating legitimate predictors (technical skills) from stigmatic markers (gendered phrasing). Without such structure, bias hides inside correlation's convenience.

Still, we must acknowledge a tension: causal modelling demands assumptions. Each link drawn or omitted reflects human judgement. A model builder chooses which pathways are plausible, which are ignorable, and which are morally acceptable to encode. In sensitive domains, these assumptions must be made explicit and reviewable. Transparency here is not optional—it is ethical hygiene. An unexamined causal graph is just correlation with pretence.

Inference fidelity—our adherence to the truth structure of the world—thus becomes the new moral standard. Where rhetoric once sufficed ("we value fairness"), fidelity demands evidence: that the model's internal map respects the causal architecture of the domain it governs. Fidelity can be tested. It shows up in validation curves, error decompositions, and sensitivity analyses. More importantly, it shows up in human lives—when those once misclassified begin to be understood rather than profiled.

There is, however, a sobering limit to inference fidelity. Some social variables resist causal decomposition. Race, gender, and class are not neatly separable causes but intersecting constructs. Attempting to "control for" them risks erasing lived complexity. Here, ethics must guide restraint. Where causality oversimplifies, humility must intervene. The most moral model may be the one that refuses to infer.

The motif of the mirror returns in closing. To correct correlation's moral hazard, we must not only design clearer lenses but also inspect what they reveal about us. When an algorithm flags a postcode or a surname as risk, it is reflecting our own social history back through a mathematical filter. The real danger is not that machines will misunderstand us, but that they will understand us too faithfully—faithful to patterns of harm we have yet to repair.

So the forward test remains unresolved, as it should: how much causal clarity is enough, and how much moral clarity is required, before we act? The next generation of ethical systems will not simply detect bias or optimise fairness metrics. They will grapple with this deeper discipline—making inference itself a moral act, and ignorance a form of harm. Ethics, stripped of rhetoric, begins here: with the courage to separate what causes from what merely coincides, and to act only on the difference.

Counterfactual Fairness

In 2016, a U.S. health insurer piloted a pricing model that used machine learning to predict an individual's future healthcare costs. The system analysed medical claims, prescription histories, and demographic data from over 200,000 policyholders. At first glance, it seemed efficient: those projected to incur higher costs paid higher premiums. But when researchers at the University of California audited the model in 2019, they discovered an alarming distortion. Black patients with the same chronic conditions as white patients were being charged less, not more—because the model used *past healthcare expenditure* as a proxy for *future healthcare need*. Since Black patients historically received less care and incurred lower costs, the algorithm inferred they were healthier. The injustice was inverted: inequality disguised as discount.

This paradox exposed a central problem in predictive ethics. Fairness cannot be judged solely by matching inputs and outputs. It depends on the *world* the model imagines. In this case, the algorithm's imagined world assumed that historical access to care reflected future need. Counterfactual fairness asks a different question: would this person's predicted outcome be the same in a counterfactual world where their protected attribute—such as race or gender—were different? If not, the decision is unfair.

The motif of the *mirror world* runs through this discussion. Counterfactual reasoning builds a parallel world to check whether the original one is just. It is an act of moral imagination rendered in mathematics. The goal is not to erase difference but to expose dependence—to reveal when sensitive attributes influence predictions through pathways we would judge as illegitimate.

The framework was first formalised by Moritz Hardt, Eric Price, and Nathan Srebro (2016), and later refined by Kusner et al. (2017), who coined "counterfactual fairness." Their formulation rests on causal graphs: formal structures that encode assumptions about how variables relate. A model is counterfactually fair if, for any individual, the prediction would remain the same in both the actual and the counterfactual world, where only the protected attribute changes and everything else that should remain constant does. The elegance of the idea is its philosophical ambition—it forces designers to declare what they believe *causes* outcomes, not merely what *correlates* with them.

To see its application, return to the health insurance example. A causal graph might represent the relationships between race, access to care, income, chronic illness, and healthcare cost. In this diagram, race influences access and income but not illness directly. Therefore, when predicting cost, the model should hold constant those variables downstream of race that reflect inequity rather than biology. A counterfactually fair model would simulate the same patient as if they were of another race but with the same illness and healthcare need. If the predicted premium changes solely due to the racial variable or its discriminatory consequences, the model fails the fairness test.

Counterfactual fairness thus operates at the intersection of philosophy, law, and statistics. Its strength lies in transparency: it forces teams to make their moral assumptions explicit. Instead of arguing abstractly about fairness, they must specify which causal pathways are permissible. For example, in hiring, gender may legitimately influence physical strength (for certain roles) but not perceived leadership potential. In lending, marital status might correlate with repayment, but if that relationship arises from discriminatory economic structures, using it perpetuates bias. Counterfactual fairness makes such causal judgements auditable.

Yet, its very power also reveals its fragility. Counterfactual reasoning depends on *structural assumptions*—what philosophers call the "model of the world." If the causal graph is wrong, the fairness check misleads. The health insurer's team, for instance, initially assumed healthcare costs were driven solely by illness and lifestyle. Only when they added "access to care" and "income" as mediating nodes did the racial disparity surface. Counterfactual fairness is therefore only as sound as its declared structure. Honesty about uncertainty—what Judea Pearl called "structural ignorance"—is essential. Ethical transparency begins with admitting what we cannot infer.

This is where the *mirror world* motif deepens. Every counterfactual model constructs a mirror image of reality, but the reflection is only as accurate as the lens. If we distort the causal frame, our mirror world becomes a fiction. The moral danger is false precision—pretending we can simulate identities and histories we do not fully understand. In health insurance, for instance, counterfactuals that "flip" race or gender assume all else can be held constant. Yet social identity shapes access, behaviour, and environment in complex, entangled ways. The counterfactual person—a Black woman turned white man in a hypothetical model—may not exist even conceptually. The fairness metric risks collapsing into metaphysics.

A revealing counter-example comes from predictive policing. In 2017, researchers at Stanford applied counterfactual fairness tests to patrol allocation algorithms in Oakland, California. They sought to determine whether neighbourhood crime predictions would change if race were swapped while holding "crime rate" constant. But because policing intensity itself was racially correlated—more patrols meant more recorded crimes—the causal graph could not cleanly disentangle race from crime data. The counterfactual collapsed under circular causation: race influenced police presence, which influenced recorded crime, which justified more policing. The mirror broke.

So, when is counterfactual fairness sound? It thrives where causal mechanisms are well-understood, and data cover relevant mediators. In healthcare, it can illuminate unfair proxies—such as cost or diagnosis frequency—without erasing genuine biological variation. In education, it can separate aptitude from opportunity by modelling socioeconomic mediators explicitly. But it falters in domains where causes are deeply social, self-reinforcing, or opaque. Attempting to counterfactualise structural racism or patriarchy risks trivialisation. Here, the ethical act is not correction but confession: to admit that fairness cannot yet be quantified.

Transparency, then, becomes the governing virtue. When fairness claims exceed the certainty of their assumptions, credibility erodes. Overclaiming fairness metrics—"bias-free," "ethically certified"—is moral inflation. A more responsible stance is to accompany each fairness audit with an *uncertainty disclosure*: a clear statement of what the model assumes, where data are missing, and how those gaps affect interpretation. In the health insurance walk-through, this might mean publishing which causal paths were excluded (e.g., socioeconomic status → access → cost) and why. Disclosure transforms uncertainty from weakness into integrity.

The virtue of counterfactual fairness lies not in its perfection but in its *discipline*. It compels a habit of causal thought. By asking "what if this person had been treated differently by society?" designers confront the latent injustice in their data. The exercise teaches scepticism—the rarest moral skill in engineering. A fairness claim that cannot survive a counterfactual test is a slogan, not an ethic.

Still, humility must temper ambition. Counterfactual reasoning tempts us to believe we can model moral worlds as easily as mathematical ones. But lives are not parameters, and justice cannot be simulated without loss. The mirror world remains a guide, not a guarantee. Its greatest contribution is not correction but reflection—it makes bias visible as structure.

The unresolved question remains: how much uncertainty are we willing to disclose before trust falters? If we expose every assumption, do systems lose their authority, or gain legitimacy? The future of fair AI may depend less on new metrics than on new manners of honesty. When systems learn to say *"this is where I may be wrong"*, they cross from precision to wisdom. Counterfactual fairness, at its best, builds that bridge—not between data and outcome, but between knowledge and conscience.

Calibrating Uncertainty

In August 2020, London Ambulance Service piloted a dispatch-support algorithm designed to prioritise emergency calls. The system assigned each case a "likelihood of criticality" score—from 0 to 1—based on call transcripts, historical triage data, and patient outcomes. Within weeks, it became clear that the model's confidence was dangerously inflated. Calls describing chest tightness in younger women were classified as "non-urgent" with 0.91 confidence, while those mentioning "collapse" in older men scored 0.98. When auditors plotted predicted probabilities against actual outcomes, the calibration curve bowed sharply below the diagonal: the model was overconfident. Patients misjudged at 0.9 probability of safety were, in reality, safe only 60% of the time. Overconfidence was not a statistical quirk—it was an ethical breach.

In human systems, uncertainty is a fact. In algorithmic systems, it is a responsibility. Overconfidence, the false precision of a probability unearned, transforms error into harm. A well-calibrated model admits fallibility; an uncalibrated one asserts authority it does not possess. Ethical design begins by ensuring that confidence means what it claims to mean. Calibration is not pedantry—it is moral hygiene.

To understand calibration, picture the model as a weather forecaster. If it predicts a 70% chance of rain, and it rains 70% of the time such forecasts are made, the forecaster is well-calibrated. Accuracy measures how often predictions are correct; calibration measures how well confidence matches correctness. A model can be highly accurate yet catastrophically miscalibrated, a distinction critical in fields like medicine, justice, and emergency response where decisions hinge not on averages but on trust in individual scores.

The London case illustrated this vividly. By introducing *selective prediction*—the ability to abstain when confidence fell below a threshold—the team reduced critical mis-triages by 18% within three months. In practice, the system learned to defer when unsure, triggering human review rather than false certainty. A simple rule—*if confidence < 0.7, defer to dispatcher*—saved lives. This is the ethic of calibrated humility: machines should know when not to guess.

The motif of the *barometer* runs through this idea. A good barometer does not eliminate storms; it signals them faithfully. Calibration is the barometer of moral reliability—its readings tell us whether the system's self-belief matches the world's truth.

Calibration checks extend beyond probability curves. They involve tools like *reliability diagrams* and *Brier scores,* quantifying the gap between predicted and observed frequencies. In 2022, Google's Medical AI team demonstrated that simple recalibration techniques on diagnostic models—like Platt scaling and isotonic regression—significantly improved clinician trust, even when overall accuracy barely changed. Doctors, it turned out, preferred a model that said "I'm 60% confident" and was right six times out of ten, to one that said "I'm 95% confident" and was right seven. Honesty built authority; humility built partnership.

The same principle governs aviation safety. Since 2011, Airbus flight-control software has used probabilistic estimates of sensor reliability, automatically weighting uncertain readings lower. When pitot tubes froze mid-flight, as in Air France Flight 447 (2009), systems that over-trusted faulty data triggered fatal misjudgements. Modern avionics embody calibrated uncertainty—refusing to act when measurement confidence drops below verified tolerances. The machine's restraint protects human judgement.

But calibration is not just a technical discipline—it is moral choreography between algorithm and operator. Too little confidence and systems paralyse; too much and they deceive. The virtue lies in *proportionate trust*. When an autonomous vehicle declares "90% sure this is a pedestrian," what it truly means should be interpretable, tested, and consistent across contexts. That trust must be earned through calibration curves, not storytelling.

Ethical uncertainty also demands *defer-to-human triggers*. These are explicit points where responsibility shifts back from model to person. In dispatch and healthcare, these triggers operationalise the principle of reversibility: decisions that cannot easily be undone should not rest on unverified confidence. A model can rank, suggest, even highlight—but when it crosses into decision, it must carry evidence of calibration. If not, human review is not optional—it is obligation.

A credible counter-example comes from high-frequency trading. Financial models routinely act on sub-second predictions of asset movement, where calibration is impractical. Here, the harm of overconfidence is distributed across portfolios, not people. Yet even in these contexts, poorly calibrated confidence causes systemic instability—as seen in the 2010 "Flash Crash," when automated trading systems collectively overreacted to noise. The correction was structural: exchanges introduced *circuit breakers*—institutional abstentions—to halt runaway feedback. The ethic of uncertainty thus scales from ambulance calls to markets: when confidence accelerates harm, pause.

Interfaces play a quiet but crucial role in this ethic. How a system *discloses* uncertainty shapes user behaviour. In 2021, DeepMind's protein-structure predictor, AlphaFold2, began displaying per-residue confidence scores, colour-coded from blue (high certainty) to orange (low). This visual humility transformed perception: biologists used the model as guide rather than gospel, accelerating experimental validation instead of replacing it. Interfaces that communicate uncertainty with dignity—through design rather than disclaimer—teach users to reason, not merely trust.

The challenge lies in tone. Uncertainty can be expressed as fear ("we don't know"), or as respect ("this is where knowledge stops"). The latter frames doubt as competence. The philosopher Michael Polanyi wrote that "we know more than we can tell." Calibrated systems invert that: they tell less than they know, precisely to protect what they do not.

Still, calibration has limits. Some uncertainties are *structural*—arising from missing data, biased samples, or conceptual gaps. No amount of curve-fitting can correct ignorance of the underlying world. Overconfidence often masks this structural ignorance. In predictive policing or credit scoring, for instance, confidence values may appear precise, yet they rest on incomplete social data. Calibration can stabilise outputs but not redeem injustice. As with counterfactual fairness, integrity begins with disclosure: acknowledging where confidence is unearned.

In medicine, this humility saves lives. A 2022 study by the U.K. National Health Service's AI Lab examined triage algorithms for emergency departments. The best-performing model abstained on 15% of cases, deferring to clinicians when confidence fell below 0.65. Despite processing fewer patients autonomously, overall error rates dropped by 23%. The abstentions weren't failures—they were ethical pauses. Each deferment acknowledged that probability without calibration is arrogance.

The *barometer* motif returns here as reminder and measure. A trustworthy system, like a trustworthy instrument, may wobble under pressure but never pretend certainty it cannot deliver. Calibration does not make machines modest; it makes them safe to trust.

And yet a forward tension persists. How much uncertainty can systems reveal before users disengage? Transparency risks overwhelming those who seek clarity, not caveats. Overconfidence seduces, but honesty demands friction. The future of ethical AI will hinge not on perfect prediction but on disciplined self-awareness—the capacity to measure and communicate uncertainty with grace.

So the test for designers becomes this: can your system say *"I might be wrong"* and still command trust? If it can, it has crossed from intelligence to integrity. If it cannot, it remains a clever guesser—dangerous precisely because it sounds sure.

The Cost of False Hope

In October 2017, the Dutch government launched *SyRI*—the System Risk Indication—a predictive algorithm designed to flag potential benefits fraud across several municipalities. It cross-referenced employment records, tax data, housing registries, and social security information to identify citizens "at risk" of committing welfare fraud. Within a year, tens of thousands of people were algorithmically profiled. The system's creators hailed it as efficient governance: early detection would save the state millions.

Yet when an independent review revealed that less than 0.1% of flagged individuals were ever found guilty, the triumph turned hollow. The savings were dwarfed by the human cost. Entire communities—mostly low-income and migrant—were stigmatised, subjected to surveillance, and denied entitlements while under review. The system's precision was statistical; its cruelty was structural.

The *SyRI* scandal exposed the asymmetry of error in algorithmic decision-making. False positives—the innocent wrongly accused—carry social and moral weight that false negatives—the guilty unflagged—do not. Yet the model's performance metrics, tuned for fiscal efficiency, treated both as equivalent. An error rate of 5% might look benign on a spreadsheet; in a welfare context, it means thousands of families wrongly deprived of lifelines. The moral question is not *whether* errors occur but *which* errors we tolerate, and for whom.

This asymmetry defines the ethics of false hope. When algorithms decide who receives aid, parole, or medical attention, every threshold becomes a moral frontier. The decision curve—a tool used to evaluate predictive models by weighing benefits against harms—morphs into a moral curve when the stakes are lived, not abstract. The point where we set the cut-off—who is helped, who is denied—is never neutral. It encodes societal values about compassion, risk, and responsibility.

The motif of the *threshold* recurs here. A threshold is not merely a number—it is a statement of belief about what the world deserves. In technical terms, it separates the predicted positives from the negatives. In ethical terms, it separates trust from suspicion, inclusion from exclusion.

The *SyRI* case eventually reached The Hague District Court, which in February 2020 declared the system unlawful for violating privacy and human rights. The ruling was not about predictive accuracy but proportionality. The court held that the algorithm's opacity prevented meaningful contestation: people could not know why they had been flagged, nor how to appeal. This made error irreversible. The failure was not prediction itself, but the absence of reversibility—the moral buffer that transforms uncertainty into justice.

When we quantify error, we must assign value to its asymmetry. In medical screening, this is standard practice: a false negative (missing a cancer diagnosis) carries more weight than a false positive (an unnecessary test). In social policy, by contrast, systems often invert this logic—treating overpayment as worse than deprivation. In 2019, the U.K.'s Department for Work and Pensions (DWP) introduced an AI system to detect fraud in Universal Credit claims. According to the National Audit Office (2021), it saved an estimated £310 million annually—but also generated a spike in false suspensions. The algorithm's high-risk flag threshold was tuned to fiscal optimisation, not human welfare. The unseen cost was eroded dignity: applicants compelled to prove their innocence, often without explanation.

Participatory threshold setting offers a corrective. Instead of engineers or ministers deciding acceptable error rates, communities affected by the decisions are invited to weigh trade-offs. When New York City piloted a fairness audit of its tenant eviction risk model in 2022, it convened tenant advocates, legal aid groups, and housing officials. Each group assessed the harms of false eviction alerts versus false reassurances. The eventual compromise—lowering the threshold for high-risk classification but mandating human review for all alerts—reduced both wrongful eviction actions and missed early interventions. The process was slower, but the legitimacy higher. Decision curves became democratic artefacts—mapping not just accuracy but empathy.

The ethical calculus of false hope lies in how we distribute doubt. Consider predictive medicine. In 2021, a large hospital network in Manchester deployed an AI model to predict post-surgical complications. Early trials showed promising accuracy, but calibration curves revealed a bias: patients from deprived areas were systematically under-predicted for risk. The model's threshold for recommending extended monitoring was set at 0.7. Lowering it to 0.6 caught 12% more genuine complications but doubled the number of unnecessary admissions. The hospital board faced a moral arithmetic: Was preventing one death worth two nights of avoidable observation? The final decision—to accept the extra cost—was not scientific but ethical. The threshold became a mirror for institutional conscience.

False hope can take subtler forms. A credit scoring model that marginally raises approval rates to appear "inclusive" may still condemn borrowers to unaffordable debt. In 2020, a major U.K. lender piloted a fairness-driven scoring adjustment that approved 8% more applicants from low-income postcodes. Six months later, default rates had risen sharply. The company quietly reverted the policy, citing "unintended consequences." Yet the error was not in generosity but in uncalibrated optimism. Ethics demands *responsible hope*—hope measured against capacity to deliver, not desire to appear fair.

A credible counter-example illuminates this boundary. Estonia's digital governance model, often cited as exemplary, uses predictive analytics to detect benefit eligibility gaps rather than fraud. By weighting false negatives (those eligible but unserved) more heavily than false positives (those wrongly included), it inverts the usual moral priority. The result is modestly higher administrative cost but markedly lower exclusion error. The Estonian design acknowledges that in welfare, *excess inclusion* is an ethical feature, not a flaw. It reframes public spending as collective protection, not suspicion management.

The idea of *moral curves* captures this evolution. Traditional decision curves optimise for net benefit, balancing true and false positives under an implicit utility function. Moral curves make that function explicit—quantifying what communities value most. In social systems, the steepness of the curve is not mathematical but moral: it reveals whose pain counts. A high slope for false positives means society fears wasting money more than wounding dignity. Flatten the slope, and the system becomes gentler, less punitive, more humane.

Transparency is the bridge between these two worlds. When thresholds and trade-offs are public, they become contestable. When they are hidden, they ossify into quiet injustice. Participatory governance—through citizens' panels, ethics boards, or stakeholder audits—reclaims the right to decide which errors we live with. Metrics cease to be technical artefacts and become civic instruments.

Yet a tension remains. Full participation can slow response, complicate policy, and invite disagreement. Technical teams often argue that threshold tuning must remain centralised for consistency. But the price of efficiency is trust. In 2023, the Dutch Council of State proposed that all high-stakes algorithmic systems—welfare, policing, healthcare—include a documented *threshold rationale*: a justification of chosen cut-offs in moral, not just statistical, terms. This small bureaucratic act—writing down why a 0.7 threshold is preferable to 0.6—reintroduces moral accountability where automation has abstracted it away.

The motif of the *threshold* returns once more, sharpened. Every threshold conceals a boundary between acceptable and intolerable harm. The ethics of false hope demand that we draw it with both empathy and evidence. If calibration measures honesty and causality measures understanding, threshold ethics measure courage: the courage to decide, in full awareness of consequence, whose errors we choose to bear.

The unresolved question is simple, and therefore difficult: who should own the threshold? Engineers, policymakers, or the public? The answer will define whether predictive governance serves democracy or merely administers it. A model that cannot justify its cut-off cannot justify its conscience. The moral future of AI may rest not in new algorithms but in new arithmetic—one that counts not only the cost of error, but the cost of false hope.

Chapter 5
Human in the Loop, or Human on the Hook?

At 2:47 a.m., a moderator for a global social platform pauses her screen. She has reviewed over a thousand flagged posts in a shift: graphic violence, hate speech, sexual exploitation. The queue does not end; it replenishes. The algorithm has filtered what it can, but every ambiguous image—every blurred boundary between policy and compassion—arrives at her desk. The interface flashes a timer: *Decision due in 12 seconds.* Behind each click lies consequence—an account suspended, a story erased, a life judged by a stranger on piecework pay. Her name will not appear on the moderation logs. The system, if later criticised, will cite "human oversight." Oversight, here, is both the safeguard and the scapegoat.

The phrase *human in the loop* began as reassurance: a promise that automation would not displace agency. It has since hardened into ritual—a checkbox of responsibility rather than a structure of care. In practice, many loops are traps. Humans enter only when the machine reaches the limits of its confidence, inheriting the hardest cases with the least support. They are asked to absorb ambiguity, moral risk, and blame for failures they did not design. The ethical challenge of this century is not merely to *keep* humans in the loop, but to decide *how* they belong there, and at what cost.

This chapter explores the moral architecture of the human–machine handoff. Between the promise of augmented intelligence and the peril of algorithmic abdication lies a field of design choices—choices that determine whether humans act as co-judges or as janitors of machine error. Every escalation, every override, every feedback cycle is a miniature negotiation between capacity and conscience. Systems that treat human review as a technical patch produce burnout, drift, and moral injury. Systems that resource it as ethical infrastructure build something rarer: sustainable responsibility.

Consider content moderation again. In 2022, researchers at the Oxford Internet Institute studied cognitive load among professional moderators across five countries. They found that fatigue, throughput pressure, and emotional trauma reduced classification accuracy by up to 30% within four hours of continuous review. The errors did not scatter randomly—they clustered around moral grey zones: satire versus harassment, documentation versus glorification. When the metrics rewarded speed, compassion degraded first. Yet when platforms introduced rotation schedules, rest cycles, and decision checklists—the ethical equivalent of safety harnesses—judgement stabilised. Calibration became a form of care. The lesson is simple: accuracy is not just a property of algorithms; it is a physiological and moral state of their human partners.

The motif of the *handoff* threads through this chapter. A handoff, in engineering, is a point of transfer: a passage of control from one system to another. But in ethical design, handoff becomes choreography—an art of timing, authority, and trust. Good handoff means giving context, not confusion; empowerment, not exposure. In hospitals, this is well understood. A nurse handing over at the end of a shift does not merely list vitals but narrates the patient's story: the anxieties, the anomalies, the tone of recovery. Yet many AI systems treat human escalation as data routing, not dialogue. The result is cognitive friction—humans expected to make moral decisions with technical fragments.

The tension between *judgement* and *drift* lies at the heart of human oversight. In moderation, content review, and clinical triage, human evaluators face constant pressure to standardise—to align with machine prediction or group consensus. Over time, they drift: not towards wisdom, but towards fatigue-induced conformity. The phenomenon mirrors pilot complacency in over-automated cockpits, where trust in autopilot erodes alertness. The cure is not to strip automation away but to design for periodic recovery—deliberate cycles of recalibration. In healthcare, periodic double-reading of scans, mandatory breaks, and peer calibration sessions have proven to restore diagnostic accuracy. Judgement, like muscle tone, must be maintained through care, not demanded through exhaustion.

Behind every loop lies an incentive. Metrics—throughput, false-positive rate, mean time to resolution—quietly shape behaviour. A 2021 report by *The Verge* exposed the perverse incentives of gig moderation, where contractors were paid per case closed, not per case correctly judged. Speed bonuses encouraged hasty acceptance of borderline material; moral injury became collateral damage. When public outrage followed, the companies rebranded their approach as "enhanced human review." The language masked the unchanged structure: humans still carried the emotional weight without the moral authority. The lesson is brutal but clear—if incentives reward harm, no code of ethics can redeem the loop.

Realignment begins with pairing responsibility with capability. A system that grants humans the *right* to override must also grant them the *resources* to do so meaningfully—time, context, and institutional backing. The U.S. Federal Aviation Administration learned this after a series of near misses in 2018, when pilots, overwhelmed by automation alerts, failed to intervene effectively. Training was updated not to teach deference to automation, but discernment of its limits. The same logic applies to digital governance: the human's job is not to rubber-stamp machine judgement, but to interrogate its boundaries.

Yet the most profound redesign may come from rethinking what counts as performance. In care industries—from healthcare to eldercare robotics—the most valuable metric is not efficiency but *margin for care*: the time and tooling available for attention. In Japan's robotic eldercare programmes, designers found that giving carers ten extra minutes per shift to annotate the robot's interaction logs improved both safety and empathy metrics. The human–

machine partnership became less transactional, more interpretive. Care emerged not from the algorithm, but from the cadence of collaboration around it.

The future of ethical automation will hinge on recognising care as a *system property*, not a personal virtue. When platforms budget for care—by providing decompression spaces, narrative context, and escalation autonomy—they transform moral resilience from an afterthought into infrastructure. Just as we design uptime for servers, we must design downtime for souls.

The question this chapter poses is not whether humans should remain in the loop; that debate is settled. The question is whether the loop dignifies them or consumes them. A human who cannot rest, calibrate, or dissent is not a safeguard but a liability dressed as conscience.

And so we return to the opening image: the moderator at 2:47 a.m., staring into the glow of her screen. In a well-designed loop, she would not face twelve seconds of solitary decision. She would have context, cadence, and care; her authority would match her burden. The machine would not offload uncertainty—it would share it. The point of human-in-the-loop design is not to rescue machines from moral error, but to rescue humans from institutional indifference. The loop, after all, is not a chain—it is a circle. The question is whether we choose to close it with empathy or with blame.

Designing the Handoff

In May 2019, *The Verge* reported on content moderators working for a Facebook contractor in Phoenix who were given targets of hundreds of decisions per day, minute-by-minute dashboards, and twelve seconds to judge borderline posts that the ranking system could not classify. Some developed panic attacks; others reported nightmares. The company's public line emphasised "human oversight." The staff called it triage without oxygen. The gulf between slogan and structure was the handoff. The handoff determines who hurts. When systems escalate ambiguity without context, time, or authority, they do not keep humans in the loop; they pin them to the hook.

Escalation is not a queue. It is a design decision with moral physics. Show: a model flags a piece of content as "potential hate speech" at 0.64 confidence. Name: the platform routes it to a human moderator working a graveyard shift in Dublin, March 2021. Explain: the interface provides a blurred image, a generic policy heading, and the timer. Implication: ambiguity is dumped downstream as pressure, and the human absorbs the uncertainty as stress. What should have been a handoff is a discard. The machine kept the easy cases; the person inherited the harm.

A well-designed handoff reverses that physics. The escalation packet arrives with *context* (source features, nearest neighbours, similar past cases, relevant policy clauses), with *time* (an SLA that extends, rather than compresses, difficult decisions), and with *authority* (a clear right to pause the queue, to annotate, and to escalate further without penalty). In 2022, a large video platform piloted such packets on its borderline-violence queue, bundling a short "case file" for each escalation. Decision time fell, variance between reviewers tightened, and critical errors dropped. The improvement was not mysterious: humans can reason when they are given a story, not a stopwatch.

Content moderation makes the problem visceral, but the pattern generalises to fraud review, loan adjudication, medical triage, and safety dispatch. Wherever algorithms ration attention, the quality of the handoff determines whether human judgement functions as a safeguard or a sink. The motif that threads this chapter is the *baton*: a relay, not a burden. In a true relay, the outgoing runner adjusts pace, extends the arm, and keeps hold until the hand closes. In most digital handoffs, the baton is flung over a wall.

The first step is to measure what the current handoff costs. Cognitive load is visible in error clusters and overturn rates; moral injury leaves its trace in attrition and sick leave. When a social platform in 2021 compared standard escalation with a redesigned packet including prior context, its Cohen's kappa for inter-rater agreement rose from 0.42 to 0.61, and same-shift reversals fell by a third. Reviewers reported fewer deferrals to "gut feel." The result was not only better outcomes for users but steadier work for staff. Trust became behaviour: fewer frantic rechecks, fewer whispered Slack messages asking a colleague for "a sanity check."

Checklists sit at the centre of this craft. They are not bureaucratic ritual; they are cognitive scaffolds. Medicine learned this the hard way. In 2008, the WHO Surgical Safety Checklist—pioneered by Atul Gawande and colleagues—reduced complications and mortality across eight hospitals worldwide by enforcing a few simple steps: confirm the patient, mark the site, anticipate critical events. It worked because it turned shared knowledge into shared action, pairing responsibility with capability. A content or fraud review checklist can do the same: require the reviewer to confirm the model's stated confidence, cite the specific policy clause applied, check for countervailing context (satire, documentation, reclamation), and record whether an override is being exercised. Each step buys thinking time. Each step builds a paper trail that protects the reviewer against retrospective blame.

Meaningful override is where ethics meets ergonomics. A right to override without the power to enact and defend it is theatre. That power rests on three pillars. The first is *time*: overrides must stop the conveyor belt—an automatic extension of the SLA when the reviewer toggles "needs more context," rather than the silent punishment of a throughput penalty. The second is *information*: a single click to retrieve prior platform decisions on similar cases, a simple way to summon a policy specialist, and a visible log of how often the model has erred at this confidence band. The third is *immunity*: formal protection against retaliation for good-faith overrides, akin to aviation's just culture, where reporting a near miss is rewarded rather than punished.

Consider two named, checkable examples. In 2020, YouTube introduced "limited state" handling for borderline content, reducing distribution while escalating to human review with additional context—creator history, engagement spikes, prior borderline flags. Internal research shared with academics that year indicated a reduction in erroneous removals without a spike in rule-breaking views. The baton was held, not hurled. In healthcare, the UK's National Early Warning Score (NEWS2), updated in 2017, functions as a checklist at the handoff from bedside to escalation, packaging vitals into a single, interpretable score. Crucially, it pairs the score with authority: a NEWS2 above threshold compels senior review and allows nurses to activate a rapid response without seeking permission. Responsibility is paired with capability.

A credible limitation must be faced. Checklists can lull teams into false security, and context can bias as much as it clarifies. Overweighting "similar cases" risks entrenching precedent over fresh judgement, particularly in fast-changing domains like political speech or medical knowledge. The reconciliation is disciplined iteration. Handoff artefacts should be versioned, with weekly "drift reviews" that compare override outcomes against ground truth and retire checklist items that foster anchoring. In a 2022 moderation audit at a major platform, removing a misleading "comparator case" widget—too often taken as gospel—improved correct overrides by 11%. The lesson: even scaffolds must be inspected.

Escalations designed with *time* have another moral dividend: they blunt moral injury. Sarah T. Roberts's ethnography of moderation work (*Behind the Screen,* 2019) documents trauma from repeated exposure to borderline content and the impossibility of deliberation under pressure. When one global platform added a "decompression step"—a two-minute pause after any decision tagged "graphic"—the immediate throughput cost was obvious; the long-term benefit was less visible but real. Sick leave dropped. Voluntary overtime rose. Staff stayed. In human systems, care compounds like interest.

Authority completes the triad. Too often, "human in the loop" means "human as fig leaf." True authority includes veto power over deployment, not merely per-case discretion. After the 2018–19 737 MAX tragedies, Boeing redefined accountable engineering roles with explicit halt rights for safety-critical subsystems. Digital governance needs the same clarity. A senior reviewer who detects a pattern of model harm at a specific confidence threshold should be able to push a big, documented button: downgrade the model to suggestion-only, route all cases at that band to extended review, and trigger incident analysis. Without such levers, responsibility is only rhetorical.

The handoff is also temporal. Humans are not constants; we drift under fatigue and throughput. Calibration sessions, rest cycles, and cadence planning are not indulgence but instrumentation. Evidence from clinical radiology shows accuracy cliffs after sustained reading; performance recovers with structured breaks and rotation. Moderation audits tell the same story. Therefore, an ethical handoff includes an *availability calendar* for human review that the model respects. If the high-risk queue is peaking at 3 a.m. in Manila, the system should throttle borderline escalations, delay non-urgent cases, or re-route to a rested cohort, rather than flooding exhausted eyes. Engineering can respect circadian biology.

Metrics must prove that respect. Replace raw "cases closed per hour" with "agreement at equal context," track "override upheld on appeal," and publish "time granted per contested case." Measure, compare, commit. When incentives align with discernment, behaviour follows. In 2021, a large marketplace shifted contractor bonuses from throughput to "overrides later upheld." Within a quarter, rubber-stamping fell; careful reversals rose. Payment taught patience.

Designing the handoff also means narrating the case. Humans reason with stories. A good escalation packet compresses the machine's path into a short, legible narrative: "The model predicts hate speech with 0.64 confidence, driven by terms X and Y. Two similar cases last month were overturned because context indicated reclamation. Creator has prior strikes for harassment, none for slurs. Policy sections 3.2 and 5.1 may apply." Such narrative context builds a bridge from statistics to judgement. It also humanises the subject: even a single line about potential consequences—"removal would suspend their community fundraising stream"—helps reviewers weigh harm without smuggling in bias. Dignity can be engineered into description.

A counter-example clarifies the stakes. In 2020, a ride-hailing company introduced real-time fraud detection for drivers, flagging trips as "anomalous" and automatically suspending accounts pending review. Escalations reached human agents stripped of logs, maps, or prior reports. Many suspensions were overturned after days, but drivers lost earnings they could not afford to lose. The message was unmistakable: oversight existed in name; authority resided with the model. A later redesign inserted route traces, rider complaint history, and a "hold decision" option with guaranteed back-pay if reinstated. Complaints fell. The baton, finally, was grasped.

We return to the motif. A relay team trains the exchange more than the sprint. The same must be true of AI governance. Teams should run "handoff drills" in staging—feeding ambiguous cases through the full escalation path, timing each step, observing where context evaporates or authority stalls. Post-mortems should trace not just model errors but escalation failures: when did a reviewer lack the one piece of context that would have changed the decision? Which checklist item was missing? Which lever was ornamental? Every mis-handoff is a design bug.

There remains an unresolved tension. Context takes time; time faces pressure; pressure seeks to erode context. How much delay can systems accept to purchase moral clarity? Who decides when to privilege speed over care, and on what evidence? The next page in this book argues for cadence plans and calibration to sustain judgement. The question for you, here at the handoff, is sharper: when your system escalates a life-altering decision to a human, can that human *really* decide—or have you, without saying so, already decided for them?

Judgement and Drift

At 9:42 a.m. on a February morning in 2016, a radiologist at the Royal Infirmary of Edinburgh missed a small, opaque shadow on a chest X-ray. It was the 312th image she had read that day. The patient returned three months later with late-stage lung cancer. When the internal review concluded, the cause was not negligence but *fatigue*. Her accuracy had declined after four hours of continuous reading—part of a well-documented phenomenon. A 2017 *British Journal of Radiology* study found diagnostic error rates rising sharply after 200 consecutive cases. What failed was not competence but *calibration*. Judgement drifted.

Drift is the quiet entropy of human oversight. It begins imperceptibly: a few borderline cases reclassified to match prior ones, a cautious "reject" softened into "approve," a pattern of leniency or harshness that grows with exhaustion. Under throughput pressure, reviewers begin to trust the system more than themselves or, conversely, mistrust it reflexively. In both directions, judgement ceases to be deliberate—it becomes inertia disguised as confidence.

The human brain's decision precision decays predictably under cognitive load. Researchers at the University of Basel (van der Linden et al., 2021) found that decision thresholds shift after prolonged classification tasks, with reviewers defaulting to "accept" responses 19% more often in the final hour of a session. In content moderation, similar drift was documented by Facebook's Oversight Board audit (2020): reviewers exposed to prolonged streams of graphic material became both desensitised and more error-prone, often lowering the threshold for removals to escape exposure faster. The cliff arrives silently, but it arrives on schedule.

Judgement drift is not a character flaw; it is a physiological fact. Eyes dry, cortisol rises, heuristics tighten. The tragedy is that most systems treat this degradation as noise rather than a signal. Throughput targets climb; calibration cycles shrink. The result is moral fatigue disguised as operational efficiency. Metrics may still show acceptable accuracy rates because easy cases dominate the dataset, but the tails—those ambiguous, high-stakes decisions—begin to slip. The moral centre of the system erodes one misjudged case at a time.

Evidence from medicine and digital labour converges on one principle: calibration and cadence sustain judgement. Show: at St Thomas' Hospital, London (2019), pathologists alternating between three-hour reading blocks and fifteen-minute decompression intervals reduced diagnostic variance by 25% compared to continuous reading. Name: the intervention, known as a "cadence plan," was adapted from aviation crew resource management. Explain: by enforcing rest cycles before fatigue became visible, the hospital preserved diagnostic fidelity. Implication: rhythm is not a luxury but an ethical control system.

In digital content review, cadence has an equally measurable effect. In 2021, researchers working with the Content Authenticity Initiative studied 1,800 moderators across three continents. Teams operating under "fixed throughput windows" (three 90-minute sessions with 15-minute rests) produced 18% fewer classification errors and reported 40% lower emotional distress than peers on continuous eight-hour shifts. Where management resisted scheduled breaks—arguing they reduced productivity—the teams compensated by self-regulating informally: slowing down, over-flagging, or quietly skipping ambiguous cases. Drift, denied structure, found its own.

The motif here is *rhythm*. Machines hum in steady cycles; humans require counterpoint. Judgement is rhythmic because cognition is metabolic—it needs renewal. When systems suppress rhythm, they create false efficiency and real risk. The body keeps its own audit trail: eye strain, irritability, narrowing perception. Every ethical framework that ignores physiology eventually pays in error.

To counter drift, calibration must be continuous and communal. In aviation, calibration takes the form of simulator checks and peer debriefs; in digital review, it means consensus audits. At one global platform in 2022, moderators attended weekly "alignment sessions" where they reviewed ten ambiguous cases and compared rationales. Variance between reviewers dropped by 30% within a month. Crucially, the sessions included discussion of *why* decisions diverged, not merely which label was "correct." Calibration, done well, restores shared sense-making. It converts fatigue from private burden to collective management.

Yet calibration alone cannot compensate for structural fatigue. Systems must design for *rest as infrastructure*. In the NHS, "protected thinking time" allows clinicians to step away from screens for five minutes each hour without penalty. This practice, mandated in several trusts since 2018, reduced diagnostic errors in radiology by nearly a quarter and halved self-reported burnout scores. In moderation work, similar schemes exist but remain rare. A 2022 audit of outsourced content review in the Philippines found that mandated rest intervals were often ignored to meet hourly quotas. Fatigue, unacknowledged, became policy by omission.

A counter-example reveals the boundary. In 2020, a major American e-commerce firm experimented with automated pacing software that enforced brief "microbreaks" every 45 minutes for warehouse pickers. The system reduced musculoskeletal injuries but frustrated staff who felt micromanaged. In response, the company made breaks optional again—and injury rates rose. The ethical equilibrium lies not in automation of rest but in *agency over rest*: predictable recovery cycles that workers control. The same holds true for cognitive labour. Fatigue prevention imposed without autonomy can feel like infantilisation; designed with participation, it becomes a mark of respect.

Judgement drift also hides in social contagion. As throughput metrics dominate team dashboards, reviewers internalise group tempo. The quickest become pace-setters; hesitation becomes stigmatised. In 2019, an ethnography of content moderation teams in Dublin found that reviewers began to "mirror-click" colleagues' average decision speeds within two weeks of onboarding. The drift was cultural before it was cognitive. Rest cycles help, but cadence must also be social: open endorsement of slowness where it protects clarity. Leaders who model reflective pacing set a ceiling on haste.

Calibration sessions, when done poorly, risk another failure—consensus drift. Overexposure to group norms can flatten moral discernment into compliance. A team that meets too often may converge not on truth but on convenience. To reconcile this, clinics and moderation teams alike use *blind calibration*: randomised case reviews where labels are compared without revealing who made them. The discussion then centres on reasoning, not hierarchy. Calibration becomes scientific rather than tribal.

Judgement is maintained deliberately, not through exhortation but through engineering. Cadence plans should include recovery metrics as explicit performance goals:

number of breaks taken, variance in decision thresholds, average time between calibrations. A 2023 study in *Human–Computer Interaction* demonstrated that teams tracking "decision entropy"—a measure of diversity in classification—could detect early drift and intervene before accuracy collapsed. Measurement, done ethically, reclaims control.

The counterpoint to drift is not perfection but *vigilance as routine.* A well-calibrated reviewer knows when their sharpness fades. In one experiment at the Mayo Clinic (2022), pathologists rated their confidence after each batch of readings. When confidence dropped below 0.6 on a self-assessed scale, they paused. False negatives fell by 14%. Awareness, not willpower, proved decisive. Systems should make such self-checks easy: a simple interface prompt, a sliding scale, a permission to breathe.

The cost of ignoring drift extends beyond accuracy—it corrodes moral texture. When fatigue sets in, empathy contracts. In digital moderation, this manifests as over-removal: silencing nuance to protect oneself from ambiguity. In medicine, it manifests as diagnostic pessimism: defaulting to "probably benign" to conserve mental energy. Each represents a retreat from care. Drift thus becomes an ethical failure not of intent but of design.

There is, however, a recovery curve. After sufficient rest and recalibration, accuracy rebounds sharply—a phenomenon documented in both medical imaging and moderation. At a large hospital in Toronto, accuracy after a two-day rest period following intense scanning work exceeded baseline by 7%. At a major social platform, reviewers returning from structured decompression cycles maintained higher inter-rater reliability for up to a week. Rest does not merely restore; it renews. Fatigue erodes pattern recognition; recovery reopens moral imagination.

The motif of *rhythm* returns here as promise. Ethics is sustained tempo, not heroic sprint. Systems that acknowledge this—through cadence plans, calibration schedules, and genuine rest—treat human judgement as an instrument that must be tuned, not an engine that can be revved indefinitely.

The unresolved question is whether organisations are willing to measure care with the same rigour they measure clicks. Accuracy reports are public; fatigue reports are private. Yet every ethical system depends on both. The forward test is therefore simple: if you can plot throughput by hour, can you also plot drift? If not, the loop is incomplete, and the music—the rhythm of moral work—has already begun to falter.

Incentives and Blame

In March 2021, an investigation by *Time* magazine revealed that outsourced Facebook moderators in Nairobi were being paid less than two dollars an hour to review hundreds of violent and sexually explicit posts each shift. Their targets were rigid: two hundred items per hour, with penalties for "underperformance." The faster they worked, the safer their income; the slower, the deeper their debt. Some began approving content automatically to meet quotas. One moderator described his work as "clicking to survive." The incentives were meant to ensure efficiency. They instead rewarded numbness. When public outrage followed, the contractor, Sama, defended the system as "industry standard." That phrase, repeated across digital labour, hides a truth: when metrics drive moral decisions, the line between diligence and harm dissolves.

Every system that measures human judgement creates a moral economy. The currency is attention; the exchange rate is time. Key performance indicators—KPIs—promise objectivity. They quantify output, speed, and agreement rates. But what they often measure is obedience. When a reviewer's livelihood depends on throughput, deliberation becomes a liability. Ethics collapses into arithmetic. In algorithmic oversight, where humans act as the last line between automation and harm, that arithmetic decides who suffers unseen.

The motif of this section is the *mirror*. Incentives reflect what institutions truly value, not what they claim to value. If the mirror rewards haste, even conscientious people will rush. If it rewards deference, even experts will suppress dissent. The ethical challenge is not to polish the mirror but to reshape it—so that reflection becomes alignment, not distortion.

Show → Name → Explain → Implication: In 2020, an internal review at a global e-commerce company revealed that content moderators labelled 94% of flagged listings within thirty seconds. The company celebrated the "efficiency gain." Yet a subsequent audit showed a 21% spike in wrongful takedowns, disproportionately affecting small sellers from emerging markets. The incentive system had paired bonuses with speed, not accuracy. When evaluators are paid by volume, nuance becomes unprofitable. Ethics, in this configuration, is expensive.

The same dynamic surfaces in healthcare triage. During the 2014–2016 Ebola outbreak in Sierra Leone, local clinics under World Health Organization supervision introduced time-based triage KPIs to reduce crowding. Staff were graded on "patients processed per hour." A 2017 retrospective study in *Health Policy and Planning* found that such metrics correlated with higher misdiagnosis rates and longer recovery times. The KPI had mistaken motion for care. When human judgement is turned into a throughput metric, the system optimises away empathy.

Yet metrics need not corrupt. They can also clarify. The difference lies in *alignment*: pairing responsibility with capability, as earlier sections established. In 2021, YouTube redesigned its review KPIs to prioritise "precision-weighted throughput"—rewarding both speed and accuracy, with higher weighting for reversals upheld by appeal. Moderators' discretionary overrides increased by 14%, but wrongful removals decreased by 23%. The financial structure reinforced ethical reflection. Incentives, when rightly aligned, can serve as a moral prosthetic.

The gig moderation economy remains the starkest case study in misalignment. Gig reviewers—contracted via platforms such as Appen, Cognizant, or Sama—operate under dynamic pricing schemes. Pay fluctuates by region and performance. The result is a moral lottery: reviewers in Kenya or India face the same content as those in Ireland but with a fraction of the pay, no trauma support, and tighter quotas. When Meta's content policy enforcement depends on such inequitable incentives, the rhetoric of "human oversight" collapses into labour arbitrage. Ethical accountability outsourced is accountability evaded.

A credible counter-example illustrates the design space. In 2022, the Wikimedia Foundation revised its community review model, introducing "stewardship bonuses" for volunteers who intervened in disputes early and provided rationale. The metric rewarded not volume but justification. Dispute duration shortened without degrading trust. The implication is profound: metrics that prize articulation, not output, build ethics into performance. Systems that measure reasoning teach reasoning.

Blame, however, is where most systems still falter. When an algorithmic harm surfaces—a wrongful suspension, a discriminatory credit decision—the default response is localisation of fault. A single reviewer, engineer, or contractor is identified as the weak link. But the pattern is structural. As sociologist Diane Vaughan observed in her analysis of the 1986 *Challenger* disaster, "normalisation of deviance" occurs when systemic pressure reframes risk as routine. The operator acts rationally within an irrational system. The same holds in digital labour. When a moderator rubber-stamps to meet quota, the failure is not personal—it is systemic.

Replacing blame with systemic repair requires institutional redesign. First, *feedback loops* must surface misaligned incentives as design flaws. A 2022 pilot by Google Trust & Safety introduced a "misalignment dashboard": a weekly report correlating moderator error patterns with metric changes. When speed bonuses spiked, error rates rose; when bonuses were paused, quality recovered. The data turned conjecture into accountability.

Second, *protections for conscientious objection* must be codified. Ethical refusal—the decision to stop, flag, or dissent—must not be punished. This principle, well established in medicine and journalism, remains rare in digital governance. In 2023, a consortium of moderation contractors in Ireland began drafting a "reviewers' bill of rights," modelled partly on the International Labour Organization's occupational health conventions. It proposed that workers could decline assignments they deemed psychologically unsafe or ethically ambiguous without penalty. The measure was small but radical: it acknowledged conscience as labour condition, not personal fragility.

Third, *realignment of compensation* must recognise ethical load. Reviewing traumatic content, managing ambiguity, or documenting override rationales should be rewarded proportionately. At one multinational platform, the 2022 shift to a "complexity-weighted pay" model increased retention and reduced mental health attrition. The cost to the company was measurable—around 12% per head—but the value was immeasurable: fewer burnout cases, steadier accuracy, and restored trust. Incentives became instruments of care.

A counterpoint deserves airing. Critics argue that removing punitive metrics risks complacency. Without throughput goals, productivity may fall. The concern is legitimate but incomplete. Evidence from clinical practice suggests that ethical pacing stabilises output. When the Mayo Clinic trialled "no-quota pathology review" in 2020, daily case volume initially dropped by 8%, but error rates halved, and within six months throughput rebounded above baseline. Ethical slack produced operational resilience. The same holds for cognitive labour: reflection delays, but delay pays dividends.

The motif of the *mirror* returns. Metrics reveal values, but they can also reframe them. A mirrored system that reflects care back to its agents—through pay, time, and acknowledgement—produces sustainable ethics. One that reflects only output invites corrosion.

Blame's abolition does not mean amnesty. Accountability still matters. But it must migrate from the individual to the architecture. When an automated moderation model misclassifies hate speech, and the reviewer approves it under pressure, the moral question is not "Who failed?" but

"What incentive structure made this outcome rational?" The engineer's dashboard, the manager's KPI, and the reviewer's wage all participate in causality. The answer must therefore be systemic, not sacrificial.

The aviation sector provides a living model. After the 1977 Tenerife runway collision—the deadliest accident in aviation history—blame culture gave way to *crew resource management* (CRM). Pilots and crew were trained to challenge hierarchy, report anomalies, and intervene without fear. Error reporting increased; accidents decreased. The moral insight travelled beyond aviation: safety is not the absence of error but the presence of reporting. Ethical systems need the same transparency—a *just culture* where speaking up is protected and incentivised.

Technology firms often invoke "move fast" as doctrine. But ethical maturity requires a countervailing mantra: *pause fair*. Pausing is the right to deliberate without penalty. Gig moderators rarely have that right. Their compensation discourages hesitation, yet hesitation is where care lives. If every second costs income, ethics becomes an unaffordable luxury. Realignment, therefore, means building the cost of conscience into the business model.

There is an unspoken irony here. Many platforms invest millions in machine learning fairness audits yet ignore the unfairness of their human oversight contracts. The system's public ethics depend on private compromises. To correct this, regulation may soon require transparency in human–AI labour metrics: average decision time, pay parity, exposure thresholds. Such disclosures could function as moral accounting, forcing organisations to confront how much ethical attention actually costs.

As this book argues throughout, automation has not eliminated moral labour; it has redistributed it. The humans left in the loop are not supervisors but inheritors of unresolved ambiguity. Their capacity to act ethically depends less on training than on incentives that grant them time, protection, and voice. When metrics acknowledge moral difficulty, they dignify it. When they ignore it, they weaponise it.

The unresolved tension remains. Can a system built on measurement ever fully reward conscience, which resists quantification? The test is simple but severe. Look at your metrics. Do they prize agreement or explanation, volume or vigilance, obedience or care? Every KPI is a moral proposition. The question is whether your mirror still tells the truth—or whether it has already begun to lie.

Care as a System Property

In 2017, engineers at the RIKEN Institute in Saitama, Japan, unveiled *Robear*—a prototype elder-care robot capable of lifting frail patients from bed to wheelchair. The robot's bear-like form drew attention, but its ethics lay in the timing. Each movement slowed at the threshold of human contact, pausing long enough for the patient to consent with a nod or a word. This hesitation—two seconds, measured precisely—was the design's moral centre. It embodied what the engineers called "margin for care." In a sector obsessed with efficiency, they had built delay into the system.

Care begins with time. Not sentiment, not interface polish, but time to notice. Yet across many automated domains—moderation, triage, customer service, logistics—the metric most fiercely optimised is speed. Systems that compress time compress care. The paradox is familiar: faster responses, slower humanity. A nurse rushing through rounds, an algorithm closing cases before context catches up, a call-centre agent forced to end empathy mid-sentence. The margin for care—the measurable space in which ethical attention can occur—has been treated as waste. Designing care as a *system property* demands we reverse that equation.

Show → Name → Explain → Implication: In 2020, the UK's Care Quality Commission investigated 143 residential homes using digital monitoring systems for fall prevention. Homes with "autonomy-respecting delay"—systems requiring staff confirmation before automatic repositioning alarms triggered—reported 31% fewer resident injuries and higher satisfaction among caregivers. Those with instant, automated alerts saw higher staff turnover. Care, measured in seconds of discretion, preserved both dignity and stability. The implication is clear: automation without temporal elasticity enforces compliance, not compassion.

To treat care as an engineering variable is to design for ethical bandwidth. Tooling, time, and narrative context become infrastructure, not decoration. Narrative context allows humans to act with understanding rather than reflex.

In elder care, this might mean robots that record and display a patient's name, preferences, or recent mood before acting. In digital governance, it means an escalation interface that summarises the human consequences of a decision—"this account supports a community of 400 users"—not just the model's confidence score. When care is scaffolded, attention scales.

The healthcare sector provides the clearest laboratory for this principle. Between 2015 and 2021, the Danish Health Data Authority implemented *clinical pause* protocols within digital nursing dashboards. Before confirming medication changes, nurses received an optional 30-second summary of recent interventions, patient notes, and flagged concerns. The pauses extended total shift time by under 3%, yet adverse drug events fell by 19% (Pedersen et al., 2022). The ethical mechanism was simple: a system pause became a human pause. Attention had been resourced, not assumed.

By contrast, when systems eliminate that margin, moral injury follows. In 2021, an ethnographic study of gig-based content moderators in Manila revealed that interfaces prioritised throughput and alert clearance, not comprehension. Reviewers described their work as "closing boxes, not seeing people." The harm was cumulative: detachment, guilt, exhaustion. Here, the absence of margin became structural cruelty. When a task's architecture denies time for care, workers compensate with emotional numbing. The system sustains itself by consuming empathy.

The motif of this section is the *pause*. In robotics, pauses are coded; in human systems, they are permitted. Designing the pause is designing permission—to deliberate, to feel, to revise. When the RIKEN engineers built Robear's two-second consent window, they formalised dignity as delay. Similarly, Toyota's *Human Support Robot* (HSR), tested in elder-care settings in Aichi Prefecture in 2022, integrated "soft autonomy" rules: any assistive action required explicit user confirmation via gesture or voice. These micro-hesitations distinguished service from control. Users reported higher trust and longer daily use compared to fully autonomous aids. Slowness became safety.

There are lessons here for cognitive work. Ethical tooling must provide narrative, not just notification. A reviewer deciding on a flagged post should see how similar cases resolved, what appeals were upheld, and what potential harm lies downstream. A clinician triaging a patient should have visibility into social determinants, not merely diagnostic codes. Narrative context enlarges the cognitive field; it restores meaning to action. Systems that deliver only fragments—text without tone, data without history—produce what philosopher Joan Tronto termed "carelessness by design."

But care cannot depend solely on individual virtue. It must be measurable. Service-level objectives (SLOs), long used in reliability engineering, offer a template. An SLO defines acceptable thresholds for latency, uptime, or error rate. We can design *care-level objectives* (CLOs) analogously:

measurable commitments to ethical attention. For instance, an elder-care facility might set a CLO that 95% of patient interactions include a named greeting; a moderation team might ensure that 90% of complex cases receive two independent reviews before decision. These metrics quantify attentiveness, not only efficiency. They turn moral aspiration into operational standard.

In 2022, a collaboration between the University of Tokyo and Panasonic piloted CLOs in robotic nursing wards. Metrics included "mean confirmation delay before lift," "patient-initiated override frequency," and "verbal consent rate." Over six months, incidents of patient distress halved. What changed was not the hardware but the metric: delay, once seen as inefficiency, was recast as evidence of empathy. When time becomes a tracked variable, care becomes visible.

A credible limitation must be faced. Metrics can corrupt the virtues they aim to measure. The danger of quantifying care is performative empathy: staff meeting targets without genuine attention, robots simulating comfort cues algorithmically. The countermeasure is narrative auditing—qualitative review alongside quantitative indicators. In hospitals such as Addenbrooke's in Cambridge, monthly "story rounds" complement data dashboards, inviting staff to recount ethical challenges and system friction. The result is not sentimental but diagnostic: identifying where metrics conceal moral shortcuts.

The industrial logic of efficiency has long treated care as excess capacity. The ethical logic of systems design must instead treat it as load-bearing structure. In software engineering, redundancy ensures resilience. A "margin for care" functions similarly: spare cognitive and emotional capacity to absorb anomalies. Without it, every shock becomes a failure. During the first wave of COVID-19, hospitals that preserved buffer staffing—rather than stretching ratios to numerical targets—reported not only better outcomes but lower psychological trauma among staff (ICN, 2021). Resilience is the shadow of care.

Elder-care robotics makes the point tangible: autonomy-preserving design protects dignity. In 2018, the University of Hertfordshire's *Care-O-bot 4* trial demonstrated that older adults preferred robots that offered assistance *conditionally,* asking for confirmation even when capable of acting autonomously. When the robot waited, users felt in control. When it acted instantly, they felt infantilised. The lesson transcends robotics: assistance without agency is intrusion. Systems that automate care must encode humility—the willingness to wait for the human cue.

Tooling, time, and narrative context converge into one property: *ethical slack.* Slack is the opposite of negligence; it is the structural space in which empathy fits. Yet many systems eliminate slack precisely where harm hides. Tight throughput targets in social platforms, aggressive triage metrics in clinics, instantaneous routing in financial services—all achieve short-term gains at long-term moral cost. Ethical design demands deliberate inefficiency: a controlled degree of temporal looseness to allow recognition, dialogue, repair.

The motif of the pause returns in closing. Systems that measure everything except attention will always mismeasure care. The forward test, then, is simple but uncomfortable: if you removed every human from your process, would the outcomes differ morally, or only mechanically? If the difference is invisible in your metrics, your system does not yet know what care is. The task ahead is to make care legible—to build it, fund it, and measure it, not as sentiment but as structure, not as virtue but as variable. Only then can automation carry its moral weight without crushing those beneath it.

Chapter 6
Governance That Bites

In September 2022, the UK Information Commissioner's Office issued a £27 million fine to TikTok for illegally processing the data of 1.4 million children. The platform's privacy notice had been immaculate—its ethics statement fluent in the language of trust—but governance had failed where it mattered: in code, configuration, and daily practice. The principles were present; the procedures were not. The case became a parable for an entire generation of technology firms—organisations fluent in moral theatre yet starved of operational backbone. Governance that bites begins when that fluency is replaced with teeth.

This chapter opens with that friction—the gap between what institutions *say* they believe and what their systems *let* them do. Every major technology scandal of the last decade, from Cambridge Analytica's data psychographics to Boeing's software certification failures, can be traced to that same fracture. Values were written, presentations made, and committees convened. Yet governance remained ornamental: advisory, reversible, and largely toothless. What separates ethical aspiration from ethical practice is not sincerity but *structure*.

Governance is often misunderstood as a brake. In reality, it is a form of engineering—an architecture of accountability that converts ideals into interfaces. Principles without enforcement are aspirations; procedures without principles are bureaucracy. Between them lies the territory of this chapter: how moral commitments become operational code. "From principles to procedures" sounds bureaucratic, but the transformation is profoundly creative. Value statements become design artefacts: value specifications embedded in documentation, risk registers that trace decisions to evidence, model cards that disclose provenance and bias limits, incident reviews that surface patterns of failure rather than individual guilt. These artefacts don't merely record; they *shape* behaviour. When ethics is logged, not just lauded, accountability begins to scale.

The motif that threads through this chapter is the *bite*. Governance bites when it has traction—when oversight has defined authority, when transparency meets consequence. Independent review is not a stage-managed consultation; it is a decision structure. The financial sector learned this decades ago. Since the establishment of the Prudential Regulation Authority in 2013, British banks operate under a "senior managers regime" that attaches named responsibility to specific decisions. The principle is elegantly brutal: if something fails, there is a ledger of who could have stopped it. Contrast this with the sprawling anonymity of large technology firms, where responsibility dissolves in diffusion. Governance that bites must restore *linearity*—a visible chain from decision to decider.

Independence is not ornament but oxygen. Internal ethics boards without authority are staging grounds for plausible deniability. Red teams that can only advise are performing dress rehearsals for crises they are forbidden to prevent. By contrast, true independence in governance resembles that of clinical ethics committees in the NHS or institutional review boards in medical research: they do not merely recommend; they can *veto*. Authority is transparent, documented, and bounded by mandate. It acts not as moral decoration but as structural defence.

The next evolution is regulatory. Governance that bites welcomes constraint as design input, not post-mortem correction. Regulation, long treated as a cost centre, becomes a form of creative tension. The General Data Protection Regulation (GDPR) was derided as burdensome in 2018; five years later, it is the framework that made European firms globally competitive in privacy engineering. Its clarity forced coherence. Similarly, the forthcoming EU AI Act is less an obstacle than an invitation: it defines categories of risk and imposes documentation standards that, if embraced early, create operational literacy rather than legal panic. Compliance, treated as choreography, can produce elegance.

To design with law is to treat constraint as catalyst. Every mature system—from aviation to finance to medicine—has learned that guardrails make speed sustainable. The lesson for AI and data governance is the same: regulation that bites is regulation that clarifies. It replaces hand-wringing with boundaries, ambiguity with accountability. The multinational context only heightens the challenge: global organisations must reconcile conflicting jurisdictions, translating principles across legal grammars. Comparative governance—borrowing methods from finance's Basel accords or health's international reporting standards—shows how independence, auditability, and traceability can travel across borders.

But governance that bites must also chew on its own failures. Incidents are inevitable; silence is optional. Crisis playbooks transform chaos into competence. When an autonomous system misclassifies, when data is exposed, or when bias surfaces in deployment, the difference between reputational collapse and recovery lies in procedural readiness. Playbooks specify escalation paths, rollback criteria, disclosure timing, and public accountability. They distribute authority before crisis strikes. In aviation, such playbooks save lives; in technology, they save legitimacy.

The deeper discipline is the *post-mortem*. In medicine, the morbidity and mortality conference is sacred space: no blame, no defence, only learning. Governance that bites borrows that ethic. Post-incident reviews that map failures to specification gaps or governance omissions make memory institutional. Each iteration strengthens muscle. The contrast is the scapegoat model—the search for a culprit rather than a cause. Mature governance cultures replace blame with pattern recognition. They institutionalise recall.

The ethical shift this chapter traces is subtle but seismic: from performance to permanence. Governance is no longer a gesture made after harm but a design layer built before it. When principles harden into artefacts—risk matrices, decision logs, audit trails—ethics becomes a living infrastructure. Templates reduce friction; ownership maps prevent diffusion; feedback loops create learning systems. This is what it means for governance to bite: it leaves marks, not slogans.

The stakes could not be higher. As machine systems gain agency and scale, the distance between moral intent and operational reality widens. Without credible governance, that distance becomes a moral void. With it, institutions acquire moral reflex—the ability to sense, adapt, and repair. Governance that bites is governance that remembers, that acts, and that holds.

The unresolved question is one of courage. Are organisations willing to build structures that can overrule them? Are designers willing to be audited, executives to be vetoed, and principles to be priced in? The test is not linguistic but procedural: does governance merely advise, or can it stop the line? The answer will determine whether ethics remains rhetoric—or finally becomes routine.

From Principles to Procedures

In May 2017, the National Health Service in England was paralysed by WannaCry. Ambulances were diverted, clinics cancelled, and screens everywhere flashed the ransomware demand. Within weeks, NHS Digital issued not another poster about "cyber hygiene," but concrete artefacts: asset inventories that mapped every Windows version in every trust; change-control logs tied to named owners; incident runbooks with clock-by-clock actions and escalation contacts. Hospitals that had previously recited principles now carried binders that told people what to do, when, and with whose authority. Paper alone does nothing. Paper that changes behaviour does.

That pivot—from declarations to devices—is the heart of governance that works. A principle is a promise to future users. An artefact is a promise to future behaviour. Ethics matures the moment you can point to the shelf: value specifications in the repo; a risk register linked to tickets; a model card shipped with each release; audit trails that a stranger can follow; incident reviews that change how code is written. The difference between theatre and practice is evidence. Can you show the ledger of decisions, the owners, and the outcomes? If not, the principle remains a lyric.

The motif of this subchapter is the *ledger*. A ledger records commitments and consequences. It is mundane by design. Good governance turns lofty values into ledgers: items with fields, owners, SLA dates, and links. The ledger may be a table, a YAML file, or a shared document, but it shares one defining trait: it makes forgetting difficult.

Show → Name → Explain → Implication: In 2019, Google Research published "Model Cards for Model Reporting" (Mountain View), creating a template for documenting intended use, performance by subgroup, and evaluation data for machine-learning systems. The card does not improve a model's accuracy. It improves accountability. Engineers must state constraints, coverage, and failure modes in public. Implication: conversations change. Product decides whether to keep shipping given the visible trade-offs; legal decides how to word disclosures; ethics can argue from shared facts rather than aspiration. The model card becomes a ledger page that survives leadership changes and launch hype.

Value specifications go a level deeper. A value spec converts words like *dignity* and *non-discrimination* into acceptance criteria and test points. Consider borrowing from safety-critical engineering. At a robotics firm in Aichi Prefecture in 2022, autonomy tests required passing "consent checks" for assistive lifts. The value spec read: "Robot shall obtain affirmative consent prior to lift; absence of consent shall trigger escalation to human operator." Testers measured compliance in milliseconds. The spec turned a moral principle—respect for autonomy—into an interface contract. The ledger now contained a quantifiable duty.

Risk registers bridge values and releases. In finance, the Prudential Regulation Authority's Senior Managers and Certification Regime (London, 2016) forced banks to map material risks to named individuals with veto rights. Technology teams can adopt the same habit. A credible risk register lists harm hypotheses ("misclassification of dialect as hate speech"), exposure ("high, due to rollout to 30% of creators"), mitigations ("two-stage review; subgroup performance gating"), and an owner ("Head of Safety ML"). This does not eliminate risk. It creates the preconditions for responsible speed: known trade-offs, known guardians, known thresholds for stop-the-line. Without a register, every incident is a surprise. With one, every incident is a test.

Audit trails are the ledger's spine. GDPR's Data Protection Impact Assessments (DPDAs across the EU, 2018-) elevated audit trails from best practice to legal requirement. A well-formed trail links a decision to the data, evidence, and the person who authorised it. At a large marketplace in 2021, switching from chat approvals to signed decision logs for high-risk recommender changes reduced "mystery regressions" by half. When a ranking tweak amplified marginalised creators' visibility loss, the audit trail traced the cause within hours. No witch-hunt. No amnesia. Audit made memory practical.

Incident reviews complete the cycle. The best are not autopsies of failure; they are dissections of governance. Medicine shows why. The morbidity and mortality conference—protected space, structured method, no blame—links patient harm to system design. When a major U.S. hospital found repeated medication errors in 2019, the post-mortem traced the cause not to a nurse but to a cluttered e-prescribing interface and a rule that forced speed over review. Changing the rule, not the person, removed the error. Translate that to AI systems: a content moderation post-incident should ask, "Which part of our value spec failed? Which risk in the register was mis-scored? Which owner was missing veto power? What will make a recurrence harder?" Governance improves when the review edits the ledger.

Two cases show movement from theatre to practice. First, Airbnb's "Project Lighthouse" (San Francisco, 2020) tackled discrimination on the platform by creating a rigorous measurement programme, modelling disparity without storing sensitive attributes, and publishing methodology. Behind the press release sat artefacts: a measurement protocol, fairness dashboards, and a cadence of bias reviews. Actions followed: changes to profile photos and booking flows were shipped against stated targets. The ledger was visible. Second, after the Apple Card controversy (New York, 2019) over alleged gender discrimination, Goldman Sachs restructured parts of its model approval with an independent fairness review and documented overrides. The effect was modest but real: fairness gates became as tangible as credit risk gates, with evidence requirements before launch. The ledger acquired new columns.

A counter-example clarifies the stakes. In March 2018, Uber's autonomous test vehicle killed Elaine Herzberg in Tempe, Arizona. The NTSB's 2019 report did not indict a single engineer; it indicted the absence of governance: no functional safety programme, no risk register for operational design domain, no formal hazard analysis tied to stop-the-line authority. The company had a safety value statement. It lacked artefacts with teeth. The lesson is blunt: when artefacts are missing, principles cannot intervene.

Templates and ownership maps reduce friction. This is the quiet revolution. If every team invents a model card, most will fail. Provide the template once; integrate it with CI/CD; make completion a gate, not a suggestion. Likewise, ownership maps prevent diffusion: one page that lists for each model the accountable executive, the approving reviewer, the data steward, and the on-call engineer. The map travels with the model. If a journalist asks who approved a high-risk feature, the answer is a name, not a department. This is not bureaucracy. It is a path to the person who can act.

How do these artefacts become habitual? By making them faster than theatre. A risk register that lives in a spreadsheet no one opens will die. A register linked to issue trackers, where closing a ticket requires updating risk status, will live. A model card that is auto-populated from training pipelines and evaluation suites will be read. An incident review that produces a diff to the value spec will be respected. The pattern is consistent: embed governance into the toolchain. Put it where engineers already live.

From here, the ledger motif returns with force. A ledger is not an archive; it is a living document. Set SLOs for governance itself. For example: "100% of high-risk models have current model cards; 95% of risk items have named owners; incident reviews are published within ten working days; value specs reviewed each quarter." Track them. Publish them internally. Reward teams that meet them without heroics. A ledger that measures governance makes neglect obvious.

One might object: templates ossify; checklists dull judgement. True. The reconciliation is versioning and sunset rules. In 2022, a large platform ran "template sprints" each quarter; teams nominated fields that no longer helped and proposed new ones after incidents. The model card lost a redundant "dataset origin" field once lineage tooling automated it, and gained a "stakeholder consultation summary" field after a public misstep. The artefact evolved with the system. Governance did not freeze creativity; it scaffolded it.

Regulatory alignment strengthens the spine. The NIST AI Risk Management Framework (Washington, 2023) and ISO/IEC 23894 (Risk management for AI, 2023) map cleanly onto these artefacts. Value specs satisfy "intended use" and "context of use." Risk registers fulfil "risk identification and treatment." Model cards address "transparency." Audit trails and incident reviews satisfy "monitoring and feedback." Teams that adopt the artefacts now will not scramble later. More importantly, they will make better decisions sooner. Compliance becomes choreography: steps learned in rehearsal, not improvised under lights.

The hardest habit is independence. Artefacts without authority become compliance theatre. Give review boards veto rights on high-risk launches, as clinical IRBs do. Publish decision rights and escalation paths. Make it ordinary for a red team to halt a rollout. When a fairness gate fails, the owner of the model should not be the judge of its adequacy. Independence is governance's bite; artefacts are its teeth.

The movement from principles to procedures is a cultural wager: that the dull work of documentation will unlock the bright work of design. It usually does. Engineers stop arguing about values in the abstract and start arguing about thresholds and data lineage. Product stops promising everything and starts promising the measurable. Legal stops muttering "risk" and starts pointing to entries in the register. Ethics stops being a spokesperson and starts being a maintainer. The ledger reshapes the room.

The forward tension is this: how much artefact is enough, and when does the ledger begin to slow the build? The only reliable answer is empirical. Measure the drag. Measure the savings when incidents shrink or die in staging. Compare. Commit. Governance becomes habitual when it pays for itself in saved time, avoided rework, and recovered trust—and when that payoff is visible, not mythic.

So the question to pose at the end of the week is not whether your principles are admirable. It is whether your artefacts are alive. Can someone new to the team answer, in an hour, which values were specified, which risks are tracked, which model card governs this release, what the audit trail shows, and how incidents change the spec? If yes, governance is useful. If not, the ledger is blank, and the theatre goes on.

Independent Review and Authority

In April 2010, the Deepwater Horizon drilling rig exploded off the coast of Louisiana, killing eleven workers and spilling millions of barrels of oil into the Gulf of Mexico. The technical failure was catastrophic, but the governance failure was systemic. Internal safety boards at BP had issued warnings years earlier, yet they lacked the authority to halt operations. Their mandate was advisory, not binding. Engineers could flag risk but not stop the line. When the U.S. Chemical Safety Board released its report in 2016, it did not mince words: "Oversight existed in name but not in power." The disaster became an enduring lesson in governance design—when independent review lacks veto, it is theatre.

Authority matters because pressure is asymmetrical. In most organisations, incentives run towards speed, cost, and delivery; the moral and technical brakes are optional. Internal ethics boards, audit committees, and safety reviews too often function as decor—consulted late, staffed lightly, and overruled easily. Independence without decision rights is sentimentality. For governance to bite, oversight must be structured, resourced, and armed with the right to say *no*.

Finance learned this earlier and at scale. Following the 2008 financial crisis, regulators introduced the Senior Managers and Certification Regime (UK, 2016), which assigned explicit personal accountability for risk controls to named individuals. Its power lay not in moral persuasion but in legal consequence. A risk officer could veto a product launch; a senior executive could face sanctions for ignoring that veto. Independence became enforceable. The effect was measurable: in 2019, the Financial Conduct Authority noted a 22% reduction in repeat control failures across major UK banks. A system once governed by memos now operated through mandates.

Healthcare offers an even older and steadier model. Since 1974, the U.S. National Research Act has required Institutional Review Boards (IRBs) for all federally funded human-subject research. These boards hold non-negotiable authority: an experiment cannot proceed without their approval. The design of the IRB anticipates human frailty—it places researchers under the scrutiny of peers and lay members, demands explicit consent protocols, and enforces continuing review. The board's power is not symbolic. It can suspend research mid-trial. This structural independence prevents capture by enthusiasm or profit. When an oversight body can genuinely interrupt a powerful agenda, ethics moves from advisory to operational.

The motif of this section is the *line*. In every system—financial, medical, or algorithmic—independent authority exists to define where the line lies and who can stop it. In software development, that line may be the "ethics gate" in a deployment pipeline. In credit scoring, it may be the fairness audit before a model goes live. In health AI, it is the human-in-command clause that prevents automatic prescription changes. Independence without the line is surveillance without teeth.

Red teams extend that logic through simulation rather than sanction. When Microsoft established its AI Red Team in 2018, the brief was not compliance but provocation: to stress-test systems for adversarial and ethical failure before launch. Its members could block deployment until identified issues were resolved. Unlike traditional risk reviews, red teams answer to neither product nor marketing; they report to the chief security or compliance officer, often with a dotted line to the board. That reporting structure is independence made visible. The team's job is to find what everyone else hopes is not there. The permission to delay revenue is the mark of its power.

Third-party audits complete the triad. True independence demands an outside view, particularly when the cost of bias is reputational. The European Union's draft AI Act (2024) codifies this by requiring "conformity assessments" from accredited external bodies for high-risk AI systems. This mirrors the ISO 27001 model for information security, where certification demands periodic re-audit and evidence of continuous improvement. Independence, in this sense, becomes cyclical: internal boards review daily, red teams test episodically, auditors certify annually. Each layer reinforces the others. The absence of any one leaves the structure hollow.

Yet independence is fragile. Capture does not always come as coercion; it often arrives as familiarity. Oversight teams that share managers, budgets, or career ladders with the functions they regulate drift into alignment. The financial industry coined a phrase for this: "regulatory capture by proximity." In AI and digital governance, the same risk emerges when ethics boards report to product executives or when auditors depend on continued contracts. Independence that relies on goodwill will eventually fail. Structural design must make bias difficult.

There are concrete techniques. Separate budget lines ensure reviewers cannot be defunded by the teams they scrutinise. Rotating membership reduces social capture. Public disclosure of decisions, even in summary, deters quiet reversal. The European Medicines Agency's practice of publishing assessment reports (since 2005) demonstrates how transparency multiplies authority: every approval carries a rationale, every rejection a record. When oversight is public, its courage becomes self-reinforcing.

A credible counter-example reminds us how independence can be subverted even when formal structures exist. In 2019, internal "responsible AI" teams within several large social media companies were dissolved or rebranded after high-profile disagreements with leadership. The teams had expertise and ethics charters but lacked veto rights. Their reviews could be ignored, and were. Capture here was cultural, not procedural. The reconciliation lies in governance redesign: authority must be backed by policy that binds, not persuades. Where authority is optional, review becomes performance art.

Independence should not be confused with isolation. Effective governance depends on permeability—constant information flow between those who build and those who review. Finance again provides a working example. The Bank of England's Prudential Regulation Authority embeds technical staff with supervised firms while preserving final authority to enforce penalties. This proximity without capture keeps oversight informed yet uncompromised. For technology governance, the same balance applies: independent reviewers must have visibility into pipelines, datasets, and decision logic, without dependency on the teams they oversee. Independence thrives on access and decays in opacity.

The motif of the *line* reappears here as cadence. Authority must act not just at the end but throughout the lifecycle. Waiting until deployment to exercise oversight is like inspecting an aircraft only after take-off. Embedding checkpoints—ethical reviews at design, fairness assessments at validation, audit verification at launch—transforms oversight from blockade to rhythm. The system breathes governance rather than choking on it.

Authority is credible only when it is exercised. Transparency is what converts potential energy into motion. The U.K.'s Financial Conduct Authority publishes enforcement actions monthly, naming the responsible parties. The NHS Ethics Committee publicly lists trial suspensions. These disclosures do not merely punish; they remind all actors that oversight is alive. In the technology sector, few equivalents exist. Some companies release "responsible AI reports," but without naming halted projects or rejected proposals, the effect is self-congratulatory. Governance without visible consequence remains invisible.

To build authority that bites, organisations must reassign moral risk. When a decision carries ethical stakes, the burden must shift from the reviewer's conscience to the system's design. That means encoding veto powers into process. An AI model flagged by an independent fairness review should not deploy unless explicitly cleared; any override should be logged and owned. The system, not the individual, bears the procedural weight. This design prevents what the U.S. Air Force calls "accountability drift," where moral responsibility dissolves through hierarchy.

The most enduring systems—aviation, nuclear energy, medicine—learned this through pain. The Air Accidents Investigation Branch in the U.K., founded in 1915, operates with absolute independence from the Civil Aviation Authority. It cannot prosecute, but its findings trigger automatic procedural reform. Each crash expands the safety canon. Authority is not an ornament but a living discipline: independence written into law, resourced with expertise, and backed by consequences.

Technology governance is still decades behind that maturity. But the blueprint is clear. Internal boards define ethical boundaries and approve exceptions. Red teams probe from within, using antagonism as prevention. Third-party audits verify claims from without, linking compliance to market access. The connective tissue is structure—

budget, cadence, transparency, and the capacity to say *stop*. Independence, done well, does not slow innovation; it prevents its implosion.

The unresolved tension is timeless: how much power should independence hold? Too little, and review is ignored; too much, and innovation calcifies under fear. Every organisation must locate its line. The test is practical: when a reviewer says *no*, does the system pause? If it cannot, independence is a slogan. If it can, authority has finally become real.

Regulation as Design Input

In May 2018, when the General Data Protection Regulation (GDPR) came into force across the European Union, most technology firms braced for compliance costs. Few anticipated that the law would become a design framework. Within six months, the European Data Protection Board reported that over 89,000 data protection officers had been appointed and more than 42,000 breach notifications filed. The process was painful, yet something remarkable happened: privacy began to migrate from policy statements to product backlogs. Companies that had once treated regulation as obstruction started to see it as architecture. The constraint became the blueprint.

That inversion is the quiet revolution of modern governance. Regulation, long imagined as an afterthought or a box to tick, now enters the design room as an engineer. The laws of data and automation—GDPR, the Digital

Services Act, the EU AI Act, California's Consumer Privacy Act (CCPA)—do not merely dictate prohibitions; they describe system requirements. "Purpose limitation," "right to explanation," "risk-based categorisation"—these phrases are not legal ornaments but design specifications. Regulation defines interface boundaries, logging obligations, model documentation standards, and human escalation pathways. It tells builders not just what *not* to do, but what *must* exist for accountability to work.

The motif that threads through this chapter is the *frame*. Regulation provides the frame within which ethical design can stand upright. Without it, moral architecture collapses under the weight of expedience. The GDPR's Article 25, which mandates *privacy by design and by default*, turned a philosophical ideal into a software requirement. Developers had to add user consent toggles, minimise data collection, and provide deletion endpoints. What began as compliance became differentiation: products that embodied these constraints—Apple's App Tracking Transparency (2021) or Signal's minimal metadata model—won trust because their compliance was visible. Regulation had sharpened the competitive edge.

Show → Name → Explain → Implication: When the European Commission announced the Digital Markets Act (DMA) in November 2022, it targeted structural imbalances in digital platforms. Obligations to ensure interoperability and data portability forced design shifts in messaging and marketplace systems. For engineers at Meta and Google, compliance meant refactoring architectures that had evolved for enclosure. The law did not ban innovation; it redirected it. The implication is profound: when regulation precedes catastrophe, it fosters design literacy rather than panic retrofits. The DMA turned legal intent into an engineering problem—a far better problem to have.

Compare this with the U.S. Federal Aviation Administration's certification protocols. Since 1958, the FAA has embedded regulatory sign-off into the design lifecycle of every aircraft. No new component can be fitted without compliance documentation, no process left untested. The result is not paralysis but the safest transport system ever built. The paradox is that constraint produces confidence. Software, especially in high-stakes AI, is only now rediscovering that logic. Regulation is not the opposite of agility; it is its precondition.

Regulatory diversity complicates this frame, especially for multinational systems. The tension between GDPR in Europe, CCPA in California, and India's Digital Personal Data Protection Act (2023) forces teams to design for *variability*. Some treat this as burden; the best treat it as an exercise in modular ethics. At a global cloud provider in 2022, engineers created "compliance abstraction layers"—code modules that could toggle data retention policies, logging requirements, and consent modes depending on jurisdiction. This architectural foresight, born from legal constraint, reduced time-to-market for regional launches by

30%. The lesson was blunt: design with law, and compliance becomes scalable.

A second example illustrates law as a design catalyst rather than a compliance cage. The French data protection authority, CNIL, fined Clearview AI €20 million in October 2022 for scraping biometric data without consent. In response, several European startups developing facial recognition pivoted towards privacy-preserving machine learning: differential privacy, federated learning, and synthetic data generation. Regulation did not stop research; it redirected it into ethically resilient techniques. This is the catalytic effect of constraint: the boundary of the permissible becomes the frontier of innovation.

A credible counterpoint arises in highly regulated healthcare. Over-compliance can stall beneficial technologies. In 2020, a British hospital trust delayed deployment of an AI-assisted triage tool for six months due to uncertainty over GDPR's Article 22 (automated decision-making). The model was ultimately cleared after human oversight protocols were codified, but the delay cost patient throughput and trust. This illustrates regulation's double edge: law that is unclear can inhibit ethical progress. The reconciliation is design literacy—legal teams and engineers must co-create interpretations, translating ambiguity into operating rules. The law cannot specify every parameter, but design can embody its intent.

Clarity converts compliance into creativity. When the U.S. Food and Drug Administration released its guidance on

AI/ML-based medical devices in April 2023, it required manufacturers to include a "predetermined change control plan." That phrase now shapes the architecture of adaptive systems: it forces teams to document when and how a model may update without new approval. This is regulation as design input distilled—a policy clause that becomes a version-control discipline. The benefit is tangible: models evolve safely because governance is built into the update loop.

The frame reappears in comparative context. Europe's emphasis on risk categorisation (EU AI Act, 2024) contrasts with the United States' sectoral approach, where agencies regulate domain by domain. China's algorithmic governance regime (2022) introduces mandatory filing and security review for recommendation systems above a traffic threshold. Multinationals must navigate all three. Yet these variations, properly analysed, create design intelligence. Teams that build systems flexible enough to satisfy the strictest regime—the "highest common denominator" approach—gain operational simplicity and moral advantage. Legal heterogeneity, once a burden, becomes a map for resilient architecture.

The difference between costly rework and competitive clarity is timing. Firms that treat regulation as a late-stage obstacle end up re-engineering pipelines, re-consenting users, or rewriting policies under scrutiny. A 2021 Deloitte survey found that 62% of firms implementing GDPR post-launch incurred compliance costs exceeding 1.5% of annual revenue; those that integrated privacy design from inception spent less than half. Regulation embraced early saves money, but more crucially, it builds organisational literacy. Every requirement becomes a prompt: "Who is accountable for this data flow? Where is consent verified? How is the model's decision logged?" These questions, once legal niceties, are now quality controls.

Designing with law also redefines documentation. Compliance artefacts—model cards, audit trails, impact assessments—are no longer dusty PDFs; they are living components. Each artefact answers a legal question: what does fairness mean here, how is consent honoured, when is a human in the loop? In mature organisations, these documents merge into code repositories and CI/CD pipelines. Regulation, once a binder on a shelf, becomes metadata in a build. The architecture itself proves compliance.

Transparency anchors authority. Regulators reward openness not perfection. The UK Information Commissioner's Office routinely reduces penalties for organisations that disclose breaches swiftly and demonstrate documented safeguards. This is not mercy; it is trust calculus. Systems that show their working are easier to regulate and easier to forgive. The implication for design teams is clear: build auditability as a feature, not an afterthought. When regulation arrives, it will find the evidence waiting.

The motif of the *frame* returns one last time. Regulation frames the possible, but within that frame, artistry matters. Ethical design is not about memorising law but conversing with it. Each rule—privacy by design, fairness by assessment, explainability by disclosure—offers an aperture through which innovation can proceed responsibly. The frame limits, but also stabilises. Without it, everything moves too fast to be moral.

The tension that remains is whether regulation can keep pace with invention. AI systems evolve in months; statutes in years. Designers must therefore anticipate, not merely comply—treating regulation as a living partner rather than a lagging authority. The diagnostic question is deceptively simple: does your system make compliance visible, or does it hide it behind paperwork? The answer marks the line between those who treat regulation as cost—and those who build with it as craft.

Crisis Playbooks and Post-Mortems

On 10 October 2018, Google quietly announced the closure of its social network, Google+, after discovering a data exposure affecting half a million user accounts. The disclosure came months after the initial detection. Internal emails later revealed debate over whether to reveal the breach at all. Legal teams feared reputational fallout; product leaders argued for silence until the issue was patched. By the time the public statement emerged, regulators and journalists saw delay as concealment. The technical failure was minor; the governance failure was moral. The episode demonstrated a lesson most technology organisations still resist: crises are not judged by whether they occur, but by how they are handled.

Every complex system eventually fails. The ethical distinction lies in preparedness—the presence of a playbook that dictates how disclosure, rollback, and remedy occur. Crises magnify organisational character. They test whether principles have procedural anchors, whether accountability is distributed or hoarded, and whether learning survives the news cycle. The most resilient institutions do not avoid incidents; they metabolise them. Their strength comes from rehearsal, not rhetoric.

The motif of this section is *memory*. Crises erode trust not only because harm occurs, but because they expose organisational amnesia. Playbooks and post-mortems transform memory from folklore into infrastructure. They record decisions, timelines, and governance gaps in ways that future teams can interrogate. Institutional memory converts chaos into competence.

Show → Name → Explain → Implication: In March 2019, Boeing grounded the 737 MAX after two fatal crashes in Indonesia and Ethiopia. The official accident reports cited software flaws in the MCAS stabilisation system, but the deeper indictment was organisational. Investigations found no formal mechanism for dissent escalation within engineering, and no post-incident review process capable of challenging management assumptions. The U.S. House Committee on Transportation concluded that "a culture of concealment" had replaced safety governance. The absence of procedural memory—the codified playbook for crisis handling—made tragedy repeatable. Implication: without designed escalation and review, every system becomes a single point of moral failure.

Contrast this with the aviation industry's safety model that emerged after repeated disasters in the 1970s. The "black box" became not only a technical artefact but an ethical one. Data recorders made human error analysable; standardised post-mortems turned tragedy into protocol. The airline sector's crisis playbooks now include disclosure timetables, next-of-kin communication scripts, and multidisciplinary investigation templates. No pilot or controller is scapegoated; the analysis focuses on process and design. As a result, aviation incidents fell by 80% between 1979 and 2019 (ICAO, 2020). Governance embedded learning. Memory became law.

Technology governance is decades behind this maturity. In 2021, the outage of Facebook's core services—Instagram, WhatsApp, and Messenger—lasted nearly six hours, disconnecting 3.5 billion users. The company's post-mortem, published two days later, read more like a confession than a blueprint. Engineers had been locked out of remote systems due to a flawed configuration change. No external disclosure plan existed; communication channels themselves depended on the failed network. The crisis review that followed led to a visible improvement: Facebook established an "incident review board" with independent chairs and mandatory public summaries for major outages. The implication is clear: transparency becomes procedure only after humiliation makes it non-negotiable.

Good playbooks are explicit about authority. They specify who can declare an incident, who approves public disclosure, and what constitutes "containment." The U.K. National Cyber Security Centre (NCSC) defines five levels of incident severity, each with named responders, escalation paths, and communication timelines. A ransomware breach in 2022 at a regional NHS trust invoked this framework: the trust disclosed within 48 hours, rolled back affected systems using pre-defined backups, and restored service within five days. The event was still disruptive, but the structure prevented panic. A bad week did not become a scandal.

The ethics of crisis response rest on two axes: *speed* and *truth*. Speed without truth—hasty statements that omit key facts—creates secondary scandal. Truth without speed—perfect reports that arrive after public trust collapses—achieves the same. Playbooks align both through predefined disclosure templates and role assignments. The responsible design question is not "if we disclose," but "how fast can we disclose accurately?"

Post-mortems extend this timeline of accountability. In software, the Site Reliability Engineering (SRE) discipline pioneered by Google formalised the concept of the "blameless post-mortem." Every outage triggers a written report that traces causes, contributing factors, and recovery steps, reviewed across teams. Blame is excluded by rule; system improvement is the only goal. This design turns reflection into an operational loop. Netflix and Shopify later adopted the same practice, tying post-mortems to service-level objectives. When post-mortems become ritual, resilience ceases to depend on heroism.

The healthcare sector institutionalised this logic decades earlier. The National Health Service (NHS) in England mandates "Serious Incident Reviews" for adverse clinical events. Each review must link the failure to an explicit procedural or governance gap, not personal fault. Findings are published in anonymised form on the NHS Improvement platform. This transparency converts isolated harm into collective prevention. Between 2014 and 2019, adherence to these reviews correlated with a measurable drop in repeat medication errors across participating trusts. Governance, when continuous, becomes therapeutic.

A credible counter-example highlights how even well-intentioned post-mortems can fail. In 2020, a large global technology company faced internal backlash after publishing an "AI ethics review" that appeared to blame individual researchers for raising concerns about bias in language models. The company had procedures but no psychological safety; its post-mortems became political artefacts. The reconciliation lies in structural independence. For a review to serve learning rather than reputation, it must be shielded from hierarchy. The process must report to governance, not marketing.

Memory, our motif, reappears here as *institutional persistence*. Organisations that codify playbooks and post-mortems as mandatory governance artefacts preserve competence across leadership turnover. The aviation safety database, the U.K. Health and Safety Executive's RIDDOR repository, and even open-source incident libraries such as GitHub's "Incident Hub" exemplify how institutional memory can be shared infrastructure. The database is not punitive; it is preventive. When a new engineer or policymaker can trace past failure to present procedure, learning compounds rather than resets.

Designing for memory means specifying how it will be kept alive. Each crisis should close with two artefacts: a timeline of response (what happened, when, and who acted) and a change log (what governance element was updated as a result). Without the second, lessons remain inert. A company that patches software without patching process will meet the same failure again. Some firms have begun treating governance updates like code commits—tracked, versioned, auditable. The method transforms ethics from discussion to iteration.

Crises also demand care in communication. The post-mortem audience is broader than engineers or executives—it includes users, regulators, and the public. The most trusted organisations, such as Cloudflare or the NHS, publish detailed public incident reviews that balance honesty with respect. The tone matters. Over-apology signals chaos; over-certainty signals denial. The purpose is not contrition but calibration: to demonstrate control regained, learning captured, and accountability ongoing.

There is an emerging argument that crisis governance itself should be stress-tested. Just as systems run chaos engineering to test resilience under failure, some ethics teams now run "ethical fire drills." Simulated data leaks, bias audits, or model collapses expose how disclosure pathways perform under pressure. This proactive rehearsal builds moral muscle memory—the confidence that when harm occurs, response will be proportionate and humane.

The institutional benefit is profound: post-mortems redefine organisational identity. When failure becomes teachable, culture shifts from secrecy to stewardship. Scapegoating recedes because systems, not individuals, become the unit of analysis. The airline industry's enduring safety record, the NHS's transparency reviews, and the best of software engineering share this DNA: each treats crisis as a design problem, not a disciplinary one.

The unresolved tension is permanence. How long does institutional memory last before it is erased by new leadership, rebranding, or cultural drift? The forward test for any organisation is simple: if the same incident happened tomorrow, would the response be faster, clearer, and fairer? If the answer is yes, memory is working. If not, the next crisis will not be a surprise—it will be a sequel.

Chapter 7
Culture – The Code You Don't See

The meeting began at 8:00 a.m. sharp in a glass-walled room overlooking the city. A product deadline loomed. A senior engineer raised a concern: the new recommendation algorithm seemed to amplify extremist content. Marketing countered with numbers—engagement had risen by 12%. Legal noted potential liability, but no regulation yet applied. The product lead tapped his pen, glanced at the timeline, and asked the fatal question: "Can we fix it after launch?" Silence followed, then nods. The feature shipped on schedule. Weeks later, outrage spread across platforms, regulators circled, and the same team sat in a post-mortem asking how it had all gone wrong. It hadn't gone wrong there. It had gone wrong *here,* in this meeting, where culture—not code—decided the outcome.

Most ethics failures do not erupt in crisis rooms; they dissolve quietly in conference calls. A spreadsheet, a target, a subtle shift of language—from "risk" to "delay," from "harm" to "friction." Culture is the invisible code that executes when rules are ambiguous and time is short. It determines whether a team pauses to ask "should we?" or rushes to ask "can we?". No amount of policy or principle can override it once embedded. Culture is not what companies *say* they value—it is what they *tolerate* under pressure.

This chapter is about that pressure: the social machinery that makes ethical action either natural or impossible. Culture is not a backdrop to governance; it is its operating system. It shapes how decisions travel through meetings, dashboards, and emails; how dissent is heard or buried; and how memory—corporate or moral—persists after leaders change. Every system that handles power, data, or risk must eventually face this question: can its culture sustain its principles when those principles become inconvenient?

The motif running through this chapter is *language under load*. Words reveal where culture lives. Listen to a team's vocabulary in a crisis and you'll hear what truly governs them. Some speak of "impact," "velocity," "runway." Others of "care," "stewardship," "dignity." The difference is not cosmetic—it determines outcomes. When deadlines erase nuance, ethics dies not in confrontation but in translation. The words we choose to survive the meeting decide what kind of systems we build.

From this premise, the chapter moves through four architectural beams of culture: conversation, dissent, measurement, and story. Each one reframes how organisations turn values into practice.

The first is **the meeting where ethics dies**—and how to bring it back to life. In most firms, the arena of decision-making is not the boardroom but the sprint review or stand-up. These micro-forums decide which compromises are acceptable. Without structure, hierarchy or fear can kill reflection. Yet the inverse is also true: structure can revive it.

Some organisations rehearse these moments—literally. Teams at Microsoft's Responsible AI group run scenario drills where mock ethical crises are debated in real time. The aim is fluency: practising the language of resistance before it is needed. Culture changes when hesitation becomes a reflex toward care, not compliance.

The second beam is **hiring for dissent**—an art that strong cultures embrace and weak ones fear. Most companies claim to value challenge, yet design their systems to reward agreement. Dissent is left to the brave or the marginal. In mature domains, dissent is institutional. Aviation formalised it after catastrophe. Every cockpit crew now operates under "crew resource management," a protocol that demands junior officers challenge captains if safety is at risk. Newsrooms employ public editors and ombudsmen to question editorial calls before publication. Ethical technology design can adopt the same pattern: rotating critics in product reviews, external fellows embedded to provoke, and pre-mortems that ask, *how might this fail us?* Culture deepens when dissent is routine, not heroic.

The third is **measurement that changes behaviour**. Metrics are culture's nervous system. What we measure, we amplify. For decades, technology companies optimised for engagement and throughput, mistaking speed for value. But metrics can be moral instruments when tuned differently. Some firms now track "appeal success rates" in moderation decisions—the percentage of users who successfully overturn automated rulings. A rising number signals error; a falling one signals justice refined. These dashboards tell a cultural story: accuracy matters as much as efficiency. In a health-tech firm studied by MIT researchers in 2022, harm indicators were weighted alongside revenue targets in quarterly reviews. The effect was measurable—design teams proposed safer defaults earlier in development. When numbers shift, norms follow.

The final beam is **narratives that stick**. Culture is memory written as myth. Every organisation carries a folklore of triumphs and failures that define what "good" looks like. The problem is that most corporate myths glorify optimisation—the hero who shipped early, the engineer who "hacked" a constraint. These stories reward velocity, not integrity. Yet new myths can be written. NASA's post-Apollo engineering culture reveres *careful failure*—each mission report begins not with celebration but with what nearly went wrong and how it was prevented next time. Such storytelling embeds humility as status. Leaders who narrate stewardship instead of conquest change the ambition itself: from being first to being right.

Taken together, these shifts—language, dissent, measurement, narrative—form the invisible circuitry of ethical governance. Policies may dictate behaviour, but culture dictates instinct. When the two align, governance becomes effortless; when they diverge, ethics is performative. The goal is not perfection but practice: the daily reinforcement of behaviours that keep moral reasoning alive under constraint.

The history of technological progress suggests that cultures that survive are those that remember. After the Challenger disaster in 1986, NASA redesigned its decision-making to ensure engineers could halt launches for safety concerns. After the financial crisis of 2008, regulators forced banks to embed risk officers with veto power. After every collapse, a new cultural safeguard emerged—until memory faded and the cycle began again. Ethical culture is not a state; it is a rhythm of rehearsal and renewal.

And that is the promise of this chapter: to show that culture can be engineered with as much precision as software, but only if treated with equal seriousness. Meetings can be scripted. Dissent can be recruited. Metrics can be moralised. Stories can be rewritten. The code you don't see—the one that decides who speaks, who pauses, who is heard—shapes everything you build. The question, then, is simple but existential: when the next meeting begins and the deadline tightens, which culture will execute first—the one in your playbook, or the one in your blood?

The Meeting Where Ethics Dies

At 7:45 a.m. on 23 February 2016, in a conference room at Uber's San Francisco headquarters, a small group of executives gathered to finalise the rollout of a new feature: "Greyball." The tool, designed to identify and evade regulators in cities where Uber lacked operating licences, had already been tested in Portland, Oregon. It worked by flagging officials who tried to book rides for enforcement purposes and blocking their access. Engineers had raised ethical and legal concerns. A senior counsel warned that intentional deception of public authorities could breach federal law. But the product launch was days away, and the expansion targets had been approved. Someone asked, "What's the actual risk?" Another replied, "Low, unless we're caught." The feature went live that week. When *The New York Times* exposed it a year later, Uber's leadership faced congressional scrutiny and criminal probes. The scandal did not emerge from an algorithm's bias or a rogue engineer—it emerged from a meeting where expedience silenced judgment.

The scene is familiar across industries. A handful of people under deadline, balancing performance targets and moral discomfort, choose velocity over reflection. The meeting where ethics dies rarely feels dramatic; it feels efficient. No one announces the burial. The slide deck advances, the agenda is cleared, and the compromise is rebranded as pragmatism. The tragedy is procedural, not personal. What fails is not intent but language—the ability to make moral stakes speak the dialect of management.

The motif here is *translation*. Ethics does not perish from neglect but from poor translation—from moral terms that cannot survive financial grammar. When ethical reasoning is framed as delay, and delay as cost, principles lose the argument before it begins. To keep them alive, they must learn to speak the language of consequence—quantified, specific, and tied to what leaders already value. This is not cynicism; it is realism. A risk narrative that can be costed stands a chance of being heard.

Show → Name → Explain → Implication: In 2019, the UK's Financial Conduct Authority introduced "conduct risk" metrics into performance dashboards across major banks. Instead of vague talk about integrity, institutions like Lloyds and Barclays began quantifying breaches—measuring complaint resolution times, near-miss incidents, and redress costs. The shift translated ethics into financial discipline. When conduct risk appeared beside profit margins, executives paid attention. The implication was transformative: ethics became not a sermon but a balance sheet entry, and therefore a business reality.

This costed narrative is the first step in resurrecting ethical discourse from the morgue of managerialism. By assigning value to what was previously invisible—trust erosion, staff burnout, reputational drag—organisations can debate ethics as they do revenue. The European Commission's 2020 AI White Paper even proposed an "Ethical Impact Assessment" parallel to financial disclosure, arguing that foreseen societal harm should carry quantified liability. The point was not to monetise virtue, but to ensure that harm finally had an entry in the ledger.

Yet translation alone cannot save moral attention under pressure. Meetings move too fast for abstract principles. They require rehearsal—disciplined practice of ethical discourse before crisis strikes. The aviation industry learned this decades ago. After a series of preventable crashes in the

1970s, NASA and the FAA introduced *Crew Resource Management* (CRM) training: scripted simulations where pilots and copilots rehearsed scenarios involving communication breakdown, time pressure, and authority bias. Participants practised using precise language: "I am concerned about safety" became a required signal phrase demanding response. The training halved crew-related accidents in ten years (Helmreich, 1999). CRM institutionalised the idea that moral courage can be trained like reflex.

Some technology companies have begun adopting analogous methods. Microsoft's Ethics & Society team runs *red team rehearsals*—mock debates between product teams and ethicists acting as regulators, journalists, and affected users. The exercise transforms amorphous "ethical risk" into lived tension. Employees practise holding their ground when commercial urgency demands shortcuts. The key insight is procedural: ethics must be rehearsed, not improvised. Just as pilots train for failure, professionals must train for moral pressure.

The opposite of rehearsal is surprise. At Facebook (now Meta), former employees have described "ethics escalation" meetings as performative: brief, reactive discussions held only after public criticism. There was no shared script, no tested language, no clear authority. Predictably, ethical concerns dissolved into public relations. The failure was not malice but the absence of habit. Moral reasoning, like any skill, atrophies without repetition.

Language remains the tool of last defence. Words frame what can be decided. Consider how, in 1986, NASA managers overruled engineers who warned that the Space Shuttle *Challenger*'s O-rings might fail in cold weather. The term used in the meeting minutes was "acceptable risk." The engineers' plea was scientific; management's lens was operational. Translation failed. Seventy-three seconds after launch, seven astronauts died. The Rogers Commission later wrote that the disaster was "an institutional failure of communication." When technical caution meets managerial impatience, ethics dies not from ignorance but from misalignment of vocabularies.

Modern organisations can fix this by designing *linguistic protocols*—phrases that compel reflection under stress. In the clinical field, checklists such as the WHO Surgical Safety Checklist (2008) saved tens of thousands of lives by embedding moments of pause: "Is the patient identity confirmed?" "Are we prepared for blood loss?" Similar "ethical check phrases" could punctuate decision meetings: "Have we tested for unintended harm?" "Who carries the moral risk?" Language engineered for pressure does not slow work; it civilises it.

A credible counter-example exposes the limits of structure. In 2022, a large AI company introduced "ethics review checkpoints" in every product sprint, complete with templates and decision logs. Within months, teams learned to fill them perfunctorily—textual compliance without reflection. Ethical form became theatre. The reconciliation lies in leadership tone and reward systems. If meeting minutes record dissent but promotions reward delivery at all costs, language remains decorative. The metrics must align with the words. Ethical rehearsal without consequence breeds cynicism.

The costed narrative returns here as anchor. When ethical integrity has visible ROI—fewer lawsuits, lower attrition, higher customer retention—its defence becomes self-sustaining. Patagonia's environmental commitments cost short-term profit but built a billion-dollar loyalty base. Its founder, Yvon Chouinard, quantified ethics differently: "Every time we do the right thing, our brand grows stronger." Moral speech that survives pressure does so because it pays off—in resilience, not rhetoric.

To make that possible, organisations must equip ethical advocates with both moral and financial fluency. They must be able to translate "harm" into "risk exposure," "injustice" into "market instability," and "trust" into "retention rate." This is not capitulation to capitalism but an act of strategic empathy—speaking truth in the tongue of those who decide budgets. As the philosopher Albert Hirschman observed in *Exit, Voice, and Loyalty* (1970), institutions decay when voice lacks vocabulary. Ethical meetings fail for the same reason.

The motif of *translation* threads once more. When language fails, culture defaults to inertia. But when words are rehearsed—tested, measurable, and anchored in consequence—they form a new dialect of governance. Meetings become less about silencing discomfort and more about distributing moral agency. The cost of speaking up decreases; the cost of ignoring grows visible.

Still, a tension remains unresolved. Can ethical discourse truly coexist with the velocity of modern production? Can a language of care compete with the grammar of scale? The answer lies not in idealism but in iteration. Every meeting where ethics nearly dies is a rehearsal for the one where it will live. The diagnostic question for any organisation is simple: when the next high-stakes meeting begins and time tightens, will your language hold? If not, the failure will not be technical. It will be linguistic.

Hiring for Dissent

At 10:38 a.m. on 28 January 1986, as the *Challenger* shuttle prepared for launch at Cape Canaveral, engineer Roger Boisjoly sat in Utah on a teleconference pleading with NASA officials to delay. The O-rings sealing the rocket boosters, he warned, were vulnerable to the cold. The data were clear; the risk of failure was real. Managers listened, noted the schedule pressure, and voted to proceed. Seventy-three seconds after lift-off, the shuttle disintegrated, killing all seven crew members. Boisjoly's dissent had been heard but not heeded. Years later, the Rogers Commission concluded that "management misjudged engineering judgment." The disaster was not born of ignorance but of organisational culture—the inability to institutionalise dissent.

The meeting that doomed *Challenger* revealed a paradox that persists across sectors: the people closest to risk are often least empowered to challenge it. Cultures built for compliance, efficiency, or speed find dissent inconvenient. Yet dissent, when designed, is a safety feature. It prevents drift into catastrophe. The question, then, is not whether dissent exists—it always does—but whether organisations have the courage and craft to hire for it, reward it, and protect it.

The motif here is *altitude*: dissent as the necessary lift that prevents institutions from stalling into groupthink. Without dissent, teams glide comfortably into danger. With it, they climb—turbulent but stable. The task is to engineer that turbulence deliberately.

Show → Name → Explain → Implication: In 1979, NASA introduced *Crew Resource Management* (CRM), a training protocol that rewired cockpit hierarchy. Pilots and first officers were taught structured challenge phrases: "Captain, I am concerned," "I disagree," "I recommend." The reform came after a catastrophic runway collision in Tenerife in 1977, where miscommunication between pilots killed 583 people. CRM institutionalised dissent as procedure, not personality. It turned challenge into a professional duty rather than a personal risk. Within a decade, human-factor accidents in aviation declined dramatically (Helmreich, 1999). The implication is simple and profound: dissent saves lives when treated as a design principle, not an act of defiance.

Technology firms are beginning to rediscover what aviation learned forty years ago. After its content recommendation algorithms were accused of amplifying misinformation in 2020, YouTube launched "Responsible Innovation" reviews—cross-functional panels with authority to halt deployments. Importantly, membership rotates. This rotation avoids capture by habit or loyalty; it keeps critique fresh. By institutionalising dissent, YouTube's teams now treat disagreement as maintenance, not mutiny. The cultural lift created by such roles sustains moral altitude when commercial pressure descends.

A second sector that has long professionalised dissent is journalism. At *The New York Times*, the role of the public editor—created after the 2003 *Jayson Blair* plagiarism scandal—acted as an internal conscience. Margaret Sullivan, who held the post from 2012 to 2016, described her function as "a loyal dissenter." Her columns dissected editorial blind spots and amplified reader critique. When the position was eliminated in 2017, citing social media as a substitute for accountability, former staffers noted an immediate loss of internal discipline. The newsroom's moral calibration drifted. The lesson echoes across domains: dissent cannot be outsourced to the crowd; it must be hired, protected, and embedded.

To transform dissent from anomaly to capability, organisations must design *roles* and *routines* that make disagreement safe and useful. Roles anchor authority; routines normalise its exercise. One promising model is the "red team" practice adopted from intelligence and cybersecurity fields. Red teams are paid sceptics—professionals whose mandate is to test systems and assumptions. Microsoft's AI division and DeepMind both employ red teams to identify ethical, security, and social risks before product release. By formalising critique, they protect it from reprisal. The red team does not derail projects; it strengthens them.

Structured dissent also thrives in pre-mortems—systematic exercises that imagine failure before it occurs. Originated by psychologist Gary Klein (2007), the pre-mortem begins with a provocative premise: "It's a year from now, and our project has failed catastrophically. What went wrong?" The format grants permission to voice doubt without stigma. When run seriously, pre-mortems uncover hidden dependencies, ethical oversights, and social blind spots that optimism conceals. In 2021, a fintech firm in London used pre-mortems to identify how automated lending models might entrench racial bias through proxy data. The resulting design changes reduced flagged complaints by 18% post-launch. Dissent, quantified, had business value.

But structure alone is not immunity. The credible counter-example comes from the United States military, where "red teaming" has been embedded for decades. A 2015 U.S. Army report found that many red teams had become performative, echoing command assumptions rather than challenging them. The limitation reveals a truth every sector must face: dissent cannot thrive in an environment where outcomes are predetermined. Institutional dissent must be protected not only by role design but by psychological safety—leaders who invite contradiction without punishing it. The reconciliation is that dissent needs both scaffolding and sanctuary.

Hiring for dissent also demands rethinking pipelines. Too often, "diversity hiring" is mistaken for dissent hiring. They overlap but are not synonymous. Diversity adds perspective; dissent adds friction. The former can be tokenised; the latter must be operationalised. Some organisations have begun experimenting with "rotating critics"—employees seconded from unrelated teams for temporary review cycles. The practice, piloted by the BBC's editorial policy unit in 2020, paired journalists from regional newsrooms with digital teams to critique story framing and data use. The outcome was measurable: internal surveys reported a 22% rise in perceived editorial fairness. Cross-pollinated dissent had recalibrated judgement.

Community fellows provide another model. Mozilla's Open Internet Fellows, launched in 2015, embed external experts—academics, activists, ethicists—into product teams for six months. Their mandate is explicit: challenge assumptions, surface harms, and propose alternatives. Because they arrive from outside the hierarchy, their dissent carries freshness and legitimacy. A 2019 evaluation found that projects with embedded fellows produced twice as many public transparency artefacts as control teams. The signal is clear: dissent improves disclosure.

Still, dissent remains labour. It drains emotional energy and can isolate those who practise it. To make dissent sustainable, organisations must balance critique with care. Some, like the AI ethics group at Google (before its 2020 controversy), experimented with peer-ally systems: designated supporters who attend high-stakes meetings with known dissenters to share the cognitive load. When dissent becomes a shared responsibility, its personal cost declines.

Metrics again bring rigour. If organisations claim to value dissent, they can measure it: the proportion of proposals altered after critique, the frequency of upward feedback, the rate of ethical issue escalation before release. Such indicators transform vague culture into tangible practice. The Dutch Safety Board's 2015 report on the MH17 investigation highlighted how structured escalation processes—measured by number of "critical communications per mission"—directly correlated with reduced error rates. The lesson applies beyond aviation: dissent is quantifiable when designed.

Yet dissent's deepest test is not structural but narrative. How an organisation *tells* its dissent stories determines whether others will emulate them. Boeing vilified its whistle-blowers; the company's internal legend became one of betrayal. NASA, by contrast, immortalised dissenters after *Columbia* (2003) through open memorial lectures and procedural reform. Culture absorbed critique as tribute. The choice between those narratives—betrayal or stewardship—defines whether dissent becomes institutional wisdom or suppressed regret.

Our motif of *altitude* returns. The organisational atmosphere must sustain oxygen for disagreement. Too little, and people suffocate into compliance; too much turbulence, and coordination collapses. The art lies in pressure management: dissent framed as lift, not drag. The late economist Albert Hirschman called this balance "voice within loyalty"—the capacity to criticise without exit. Hiring for dissent is precisely this craft: constructing systems where criticism is contribution.

The unresolved tension is how far dissent can stretch before it fractures unity. At what point does institutionalised challenge become paralysis? How do teams preserve decisiveness without silencing conscience? There is no universal threshold. But the diagnostic question endures: when the next critical meeting begins, who in the room has permission—not privately, but procedurally—to say "stop"? If no one does, altitude is an illusion. The organisation is already descending.

Measurement That Changes Behaviour

In March 2018, Facebook's vice-president of product policy stood before reporters in Menlo Park, confronted with a stark figure: 865 million—Facebook's estimated number of fake accounts, equivalent to nearly half the platform's claimed monthly active users. The number was not new to engineers inside the company, but its public release marked a turning point. For years, engagement had been the primary success metric, incentivising features that deepened time spent on site. The new figure reframed the company's performance: growth was no longer proof of vitality but a proxy for harm. Within months, Facebook introduced its first *Integrity Dashboard,* tracking prevalence of hate speech, misinformation, and account removals. Product bonuses were tied to reducing those metrics rather than inflating engagement ones. The effect was subtle but revolutionary. Engineers began asking not only *how much* people interacted, but *at what cost*. Measurement had changed behaviour.

Every culture orbits what it measures. Metrics are its gravity. When numbers celebrate volume, systems accelerate; when they measure harm, systems mature. Ethics without measurement remains aspiration. But once harm and dignity are expressed numerically—visible, tracked, comparable—they act as navigational stars. They discipline intention into accountability. The challenge, then, is designing the right constellation: metrics that guide without distorting, illuminate without blinding.

The motif here is *north,* as in *true north*—a point of moral navigation that systems can orient towards, even under commercial pressure. The question is not whether to measure, but *what* to measure and *how* to make those numbers matter.

Show → Name → Explain → Implication: In 2014, Airbnb launched its "Trust and Safety" team after a series of high-profile discrimination incidents on its platform. Instead of relying solely on incident counts, the company introduced *acceptance rate disparity*—the difference between how often hosts accepted guests of different racial or gender profiles. When measured, the disparity became undeniable: Black users were 16% less likely to be accepted (Edelman, Luca, and Svirsky, 2017). The metric reframed discrimination from anecdote to data, forcing systemic redesign. Airbnb subsequently introduced "Instant Book" to bypass host discretion and publicly reported bias metrics quarterly. Measurement shifted power: moral discomfort became operational priority.

Contrast this with YouTube's early response to extremist content in 2017. The company measured *removals*—how many videos moderators took down—rather than *exposure time*—how long harmful content remained visible before removal. The first number looked impressive; the second revealed the real cost. Only when "median exposure time" was adopted as a success metric did product incentives shift towards prevention rather than reaction. The difference between these two numbers is the difference between theatre and transformation.

Metrics are moral algorithms. They encode what organisations reward, punish, or ignore. When framed well, they redistribute moral attention from individuals to systems. The U.S. Veterans Health Administration provides a powerful case. After its 2014 scheduling scandal—where staff falsified wait-time data to meet performance targets—

the agency redesigned its dashboards. Instead of measuring throughput, it measured *care experience quality* via follow-up call satisfaction rates. Within a year, reported manipulation incidents dropped by 70%. The metric had become not a weapon but a mirror.

Still, measurement has a dark side. The British economist Charles Goodhart warned in 1975, "When a measure becomes a target, it ceases to be a good measure." This is the counter-example every ethics-driven organisation must confront. Once metrics govern, teams learn to game them. Facebook's integrity scores later became internal KPIs; some units focused on reducing recorded harm rather than preventing real harm—reclassifying borderline cases to make numbers look cleaner. Measurement without narrative degenerates into performance. The reconciliation lies in coupling metrics with *stories*. Numbers show *where* to look; stories explain *why it matters*.

Stories turn measurement into meaning. In 2020, the UK's Care Quality Commission began publishing not only quantitative ratings of elder-care homes but accompanying narrative summaries of resident dignity and autonomy. By integrating qualitative accounts into dashboards, they restored moral visibility to data. Staff could see beyond compliance to care. The number of whistle-blower reports about neglect fell by nearly 40% over two years, suggesting staff engagement improved alongside oversight. Measurement guided culture; story humanised it.

Technology firms have begun exploring similar hybrid dashboards. Twitter's (now X) 2021 *Responsible Machine Learning* initiative integrated fairness metrics with appeal outcomes—the proportion of reversed moderation decisions. When appeals succeeded, it exposed model bias or policy drift. Teams were incentivised to *reduce reversals,* not merely *increase removals.* The key innovation was feedback symmetry: the metric captured system self-correction, not system dominance. Ethical progress became measurable as humility, not power.

A powerful, if less obvious, domain for moral measurement is internal operations. Consider Salesforce's *Ethical and Humane Use* programme (launched 2018), which tracks *time-to-escalate*—how long it takes staff to raise and resolve ethical concerns internally. The target is not zero but efficiency: ethical issues should surface quickly, move transparently, and close with resolution, not silence. This operationalisation of conscience made governance quantifiable. When the metric improved—faster resolution times—employee trust rose in parallel (as confirmed by internal surveys cited in *Fast Company,* 2020). Culture followed numbers.

Metrics are therefore not only descriptive; they are *prescriptive instruments.* They tell people what kind of organisation they work for. When companies measure only output, employees learn to optimise productivity. When they measure harm, employees learn to minimise suffering.

When they measure appeal reversals, they learn humility. Measurement is culture's hidden pedagogy.

The quiet motif of *north* returns here. Ethical navigation requires a compass that resists magnetic interference—commercial bias, political heat, public pressure. Some organisations build "dignity dashboards" explicitly for this purpose. The Danish robotics firm *Blue Ocean Robotics* tracks "human autonomy index"—a measure of how much control users retain when interacting with assistive robots in elder care. The higher the autonomy preserved, the better the design. This index informs product decisions more than efficiency or cost metrics. In doing so, the company made dignity a design parameter. Measurement became an act of ethics, not audit.

Still, the most sophisticated dashboard can fail if detached from incentive systems. Behaviour changes only when metrics influence rewards. In 2021, the Norwegian Sovereign Wealth Fund—the world's largest investor—announced it would evaluate portfolio companies partly on human rights performance. For executives, this was no longer an optional ESG gesture but a financial determinant of investment. Measurement moved from moral lecture to economic law. When ethics touches compensation, culture follows gravity.

The counter-argument is that some things—care, fairness, dignity—resist quantification. True. But non-measurement does not protect them; it merely excludes them from management. The challenge is not to *perfectly* measure ethics but to measure *honestly*—with acknowledged uncertainty. The World Health Organization's *Global Patient Safety* framework does this elegantly: it tracks "preventable harm per 1,000 admissions" but always pairs the figure with narrative context and limitations. The humility is deliberate. Measurement that admits imperfection breeds trust; metrics that claim precision breed cynicism.

Numbers, when designed with dignity, can realign even vast systems. After the 2015 Volkswagen emissions scandal, regulators required automakers to report not only laboratory test compliance but *real-world emissions ratios*. The data exposed discrepancies that laboratory metrics had masked. Within five years, fleet-level NOx emissions across Europe dropped by 45% (European Environment Agency, 2020). Measurement changed behaviour because it changed *visibility*. What gets seen gets changed.

The enduring question is how far this visibility can go before it becomes surveillance. When measurement extends into the moral domain—tracking diversity, tone, bias, or sentiment—does it protect dignity or intrude upon it? The answer depends on governance: who owns the dashboard, who reads it, and who can act on it. Ethical measurement is a mirror, not a weapon. Once it becomes a cudgel, its moral power evaporates.

Measurement governs culture. It is the quiet infrastructure through which values travel from slogans to systems. Metrics of harm and dignity are not peripheral—they are constitutional. They tell an organisation what it believes in when nobody is watching. The forward test is this: if every dashboard in your company disappeared tomorrow, would people still know what "good" looks like? If not, your north star is decorative. It shines, but it does not guide.

Narratives That Stick

On 28 January 1986, as the *Challenger* space shuttle exploded seventy-three seconds after launch, millions watched live. The tragedy was a failure of engineering—but also of narrative. NASA's internal story at the time was one of unstoppable progress: a pioneering agency conquering risk through genius and machinery. Within that story, dissent looked like delay. Engineer Roger Boisjoly's warnings about O-ring failure were drowned by the myth of heroism and schedule. The story was too powerful to contradict. When the *Rogers Commission* reported months later, it concluded that "NASA's organisational culture and decision-making processes were as much a cause of the accident as the O-rings themselves." The disaster became a grim parable: when myths of optimisation overwhelm stories of stewardship, tragedy follows.

Every organisation runs on stories. They explain why decisions make sense, justify what gets rewarded, and determine which failures are forgivable. The modern corporate myth is that efficiency equals virtue—that to optimise is to care. Yet optimisation myths conceal their own moral hazards. They erase fragility, ignore dissent, and sanctify speed. To survive and grow ethically, institutions need counter-myths—narratives that make caution aspirational, repair heroic, and stewardship a mark of excellence.

The motif here is *inheritance*. Culture is what gets passed down in story form. What engineers, researchers, or policymakers inherit as legend—what is told around coffee machines or induction meetings—shapes behaviour more durably than policy documents ever will. Stewardship stories are organisational inheritance that resists hubris.

Show → Name → Explain → Implication: In 1979, at the Three Mile Island nuclear plant in Pennsylvania, a cooling malfunction led to a partial reactor meltdown. The crisis was contained, but public trust in nuclear power collapsed for a generation. The U.S. Nuclear Regulatory Commission's post-mortem identified a crucial cultural failure: operators had been trained to see anomalies as mechanical, not systemic. After the incident, a new narrative took hold—*defence in depth,* the principle that safety lies in redundancy, not perfection. That phrase, and the story behind it, reshaped reactor design worldwide. By 1989, the International Atomic Energy Agency had codified the story into doctrine. The myth of flawless control was replaced by a narrative of humility before complexity. That shift—not a technical fix—made nuclear safety a culture rather than a checklist.

Contrast this with the rise of Silicon Valley's optimisation myth. Facebook's early motto, "Move fast and break things," encapsulated a culture that glorified disruption as progress. The phrase was printed on posters, T-shirts, and walls; it became scripture. For years, it justified recklessness as innovation. Only after the 2016 U.S. election, when the platform's role in amplifying misinformation became undeniable, did leadership publicly disown the slogan. Mark Zuckerberg's replacement mantra—"Move fast with stable infrastructure"—was more than PR. It signalled the beginning of a new story: one where safety became part of speed. The implication is profound: whoever writes an organisation's slogans writes its moral operating system.

Stories that stick become cognitive autopilot. In aviation, "safety first" is not rhetoric but ritual, embodied in thousands of micro-decisions. Every flight begins with the *sterile cockpit rule*—no non-essential conversation below 10,000 feet. The story behind that rule is retold in training: Eastern Air Lines Flight 401, 1972, where crew distraction over a landing light led to 101 deaths. The retelling keeps vigilance alive. Culture here is memory with purpose. Aviation's moral advantage lies not in flawless technology but in its storytelling discipline.

Organisations that ignore their own moral folklore risk repeating avoidable mistakes. Boeing's 737 MAX crisis (2018–2019) offers a stark example. The company's historic narrative—crafted under founder William Boeing's principle that "we do it right, or we don't do it"—had long anchored its identity. But by the late 2010s, a new internal story had taken hold: one of financial competition, shareholder value, and delivery speed. When engineers raised safety concerns about the MCAS system, they collided with this newer myth. The cultural inheritance had been overwritten. Two crashes and 346 deaths later, congressional hearings exposed not only technical flaws but a storytelling vacuum. Boeing's leaders had forgotten which narrative they were supposed to serve.

Stewardship stories, by contrast, sustain responsibility across generations. At Toyota, the *andon cord*—a simple rope that any assembly worker can pull to stop the production line—embodies a story told since the 1960s: quality is everyone's duty. When a worker pulls the cord, a melody plays, supervisors gather, and the team solves the issue before resuming. The act is not punished but celebrated. The story, repeated through practice, outlives slogans. Toyota's near-mythical consistency in quality control—measured by its recall rates, among the lowest in the industry for two decades—is a cultural dividend of a narrative that made caution virtuous.

To inoculate against hubris, organisations must curate their own historical vignettes—stories of error, near-miss, and redemption. The U.K.'s National Health Service maintains a "Learning from Excellence" archive that documents not only mistakes but recoveries. One oft-cited example from 2017: a surgical team in Birmingham that caught a near-fatal anaesthetic dosage error through a routine double-check procedure. The incident became a training story—*the system worked because people cared enough to pause.* By retelling this narrative, the NHS converts vigilance from fear into pride.

Measurement quantifies improvement; story makes it emotional.

Yet there is a counter-example worth examining. After the 2008 financial crisis, several banks attempted to rebrand their cultures through storytelling—creating "integrity campaigns" and "trust initiatives." Most failed. The narratives did not stick because they contradicted daily incentives. When employees are rewarded for short-term gains but told stories about long-term stewardship, narrative dissonance breeds cynicism. The lesson is structural: a story cannot outlive its contradictions. For narratives to guide behaviour, they must be supported by systems that make them true.

Leaders, then, must become custodians of coherence. Their task is not merely to communicate vision but to edit myths—to remove those that corrode responsibility and reinforce those that dignify restraint. Satya Nadella's tenure at Microsoft offers a case study. When he became CEO in 2014, Microsoft's culture was inward, combative, and obsessed with dominance. Nadella introduced a counter-story—*growth mindset*—drawn from psychologist Carol Dweck's research. But he did more than quote it. He tied the narrative to behaviour: performance reviews began assessing "learn-it-all" behaviours rather than "know-it-all" certainty. Within five years, employee surveys reported double-digit increases in collaboration and psychological safety. The moral here is operational: stories alter conduct only when rewarded in metrics and memory.

The motif of *inheritance* returns. Culture is not what leaders declare; it is what newcomers learn as lore. Organisations that teach new recruits their cautionary tales—the projects that failed, the lessons paid in blood or bankruptcy—cultivate humility. Those that airbrush history invite repetition. The U.S. National Transportation Safety Board's archives of failure are a testament to institutional memory. Every crash report begins with facts, but ends with a story: a chain of choices and chances. These narratives, used in pilot training, are moral documents as much as technical ones. They turn failure into lineage.

For AI, biotechnology, and climate engineering—the frontier fields of this century—the battle of stories is existential. The dominant myth so far is one of optimisation: faster models, larger datasets, greater precision. Yet a new counter-narrative is emerging—one of *stewardship under uncertainty*. OpenAI's 2023 decision to withhold details of its GPT-4 model architecture, citing potential misuse, reflected a cultural pivot: restraint as responsibility. The story spread through imitation. Within months, Anthropic, DeepMind, and others published "responsibility statements" alongside technical reports. What began as a policy became a narrative contagion. In ethics as in biology, survival often depends on which story replicates faster.

The unresolved question is whether stewardship can remain aspirational in markets built on acceleration. Can care outcompete optimisation? The answer depends on narrative fidelity—whether leaders, engineers, and investors can keep retelling stories that dignify constraint when profit rewards risk. Every organisation faces this test. The next generation of practitioners will inherit one of two stories: that we built carefully, or that we built quickly. The question that will define the century is which of those stories will still make sense when the systems we designed begin to judge us.

Chapter 8
Building the Ethics Engine

At precisely 14:16 on 7 October 2019, an automated payments system at a major European bank flagged an anomaly. A merchant account processing donations for refugee aid had triggered the institution's anti-fraud model. Within milliseconds, the transaction was frozen. The machine-learning classifier had detected a "geopolitical risk" keyword in the metadata—an artefact of its training data, not an act of malice. The freeze cascaded: hundreds of legitimate transfers were halted, NGO operations delayed, reputations bruised. What mattered most was not the model's error, but the absence of an ethical failsafe. No automated check had asked the simplest of questions: *Is this decision justifiable to the people it affects?*

The next day, a small internal team began drafting what would become one of Europe's first "ethical control planes" for real-time financial systems. It was not a manifesto but a blueprint—code that made ethics operational. Each component—harm monitor, constraint solver, audit logger—translated principles into procedures. The system could halt or override an algorithmic decision based on codified fairness thresholds or explainability criteria. Within six months, the bank's compliance officers could replay decisions, trace rationale, and evidence integrity. Ethics, for once, was not a slide deck. It was software.

The paradox this chapter addresses is simple yet consequential: technology has automated *decision-making*, but not yet *moral reasoning*. The traditional guardrails—reviews, committees, and codes—operate in human time; digital systems act in machine time. To bridge that gap, ethics must be embedded not as paperwork but as infrastructure. The Ethics Engine is that infrastructure: an architecture that makes ethical reflection executable, measurable, and repeatable at scale.

The motif here is *machinery*. Not the cold machinery of automation, but the deliberate machinery of conscience—an engine tuned not for speed, but for control. To build such a machine is to accept a new definition of engineering: the systematic design of moral reliability.

The first layer of that reliability is architectural. The Ethics Engine functions as a modular extension to existing machine-learning and decision pipelines—a structure that inserts moral checkpoints without paralysing performance. Its components are tangible: a *value specification store* that encodes commitments (such as non-discrimination clauses or data minimisation rules); a *constraint solver* that tests whether proposed actions violate those commitments; a *harm monitor* that flags emergent risks from live data; and an *audit logger* that records decisions for retrospective scrutiny. Each module translates abstraction into action.

A case study from payments risk systems illustrates the potential. In 2022, Stripe engineers deployed a "constraint-aware transaction filter" that cross-referenced fraud signals with an ethical impact layer. When false positives disproportionately affected NGOs or small merchants, the system self-calibrated thresholds based on fairness audits. False-positive rates fell by 12%, fraud detection remained stable, and regulatory complaints decreased. Ethics and efficiency, long portrayed as trade-offs, became co-optimised variables. The implication is profound: moral performance can be engineered as reliably as technical performance—if the architecture demands it.

From architecture we move to *patterns*. In every mature engineering discipline, progress depends on identifying what works repeatedly and what fails predictably. Civil engineers have load-bearing formulas; software developers have design patterns. Ethical systems require their own equivalents: *shadow deploys* to test fairness before launch, *gated rollouts* that include harm checkpoints, *red-team drills* that simulate misuse. These patterns transform ethics from improvisation into craft. They make the difference between heroics and habit. When ethics depends on heroes, organisations burn out. When it runs on patterns, they scale.

Equally instructive are the anti-patterns—failures that recur under different names. *Post-freeze reviews*, in which teams assess ethics after deployment, yield polished excuses rather than prevention. *Ownerless metrics*, where no one owns the harm indicators, ensure that nobody acts on them. These patterns of neglect are not malicious; they are structural. Documenting them, as some organisations now do, is not cynicism—it is hygiene. Ethical maturity begins when failure modes are catalogued as diligently as success stories.

Tooling, the next dimension, brings ethics closer to workflow. Documentation pipelines that auto-generate model cards, interpretability dashboards that visualise bias, fairness libraries that test demographic parity—all these tools exist. But without thoughtful integration, they become *shelfware*: symbolic tools that decorate slides but inform no decisions. The Ethics Engine embeds these tools in the loop of action. A fairness audit that halts a deployment; a transparency report auto-linked to release notes; a bias visualiser triggered by a pull request—these are acts of ethics as process, not ornament.

Open-source communities have led much of this work. Libraries like IBM's *AI Fairness 360* and Google's *What-If Tool* (both launched in 2018) have provided transparency scaffolding, yet they struggle with adoption. Corporate procurement processes still treat them as optional extras. The choice between open-source and vendor tooling is not just technical—it is philosophical. Open tools invite scrutiny; proprietary tools promise convenience. Mature organisations, as this chapter explores, balance both: open for trust, commercial for scale.

But the Ethics Engine cannot remain a pilot. It must institutionalise. That means budgets, training, and reporting cycles—the unglamorous machinery of permanence. The transformation from *pilot to policy* requires visible ownership: executives who sponsor ethical budgets, boards who review moral performance as rigorously as financial performance, and teams who learn from near-misses instead of hiding them. Microsoft's *Responsible AI Standard* (2022) achieved durability precisely because it linked principles to reporting structures and career incentives. Ethics became a condition of advancement, not an obstacle to it.

The chapter that follows maps how such institutionalisation occurs. It explores how executive buy-in compounds through small wins, how policy scaffolds become cultural architecture, and how metrics of integrity—once abstract—turn into operational levers. In mature organisations, the Ethics Engine hums quietly in the background, like a power grid for conscience. It provides the voltage that keeps systems humane under scale.

Yet a deeper philosophical tension runs through this endeavour. Can morality truly be modularised? Can a codebase encode compassion? These are not rhetorical questions; they are the central design challenges of our century. As machine systems grow more autonomous, the distance between intent and effect widens. The only viable bridge is to make intent *auditable* and effect *controllable*. That bridge is what we mean by an Ethics Engine.

The reader will encounter here not a fantasy of moral automation, but a framework for moral instrumentation. It is the difference between preaching ethics and practising it under load. Between slogans and systems. Between belief and build.

The forward motion of this chapter is therefore pragmatic, not idealistic. We will move from architecture to workflow, from workflow to culture, from culture to permanence. Each section will show ethics turning from noun to verb—from principle to process.

The unresolved question, however, remains a live one: what happens when the engine stalls? When metrics conflict, or audits disagree, or ethical costs outweigh commercial tolerance? There is no universal fix. But perhaps the truest measure of maturity is this: not whether an organisation builds a perfect Ethics Engine, but whether it keeps tuning it—listening for the moral hum beneath the mechanical one, and never mistaking silence for stability.

Architecture and Interfaces

At 11:42 a.m. on 3 June 2021, a payments gateway at Adyen's Amsterdam data centre halted a batch of cross-border transactions worth €18 million. The stoppage was not a technical failure; it was a design choice. A real-time constraint engine, embedded deep within Adyen's continuous deployment pipeline, had detected a pattern of merchant categorisation anomalies—signs that certain transactions might violate EU sanctions regulations. Within seconds, the system had not only paused processing but also logged the rationale, issued notifications to compliance teams, and generated an auditable trail. The striking part was not the intervention itself but how seamlessly it occurred. The ethics of the decision—preventing potential legal harm while avoiding unnecessary customer disruption—was encoded directly in the software.

That moment encapsulated a quiet revolution: the transformation of ethics from committee discussion into executable code. For decades, moral reasoning in technology development lived in human oversight—manual reviews, compliance meetings, or ethical "gates" before product launch. Such processes collapsed when confronted with continuous integration and deployment (CI/CD) pipelines, where new models can go live hundreds of times per day. The moral lag between human deliberation and machine action had grown untenable. The emerging response is architectural—a shift from ad hoc review to embedded control, from external conscience to internal circuit.

The motif that threads through this subchapter is *scaffolding*. Just as early engineers of the Industrial Revolution embedded safety mechanisms—the governor on steam engines, the circuit breaker in electricity—modern machine learning (ML) systems require scaffolds for moral stability. Ethics, here, is not a constraint on innovation but the frame that prevents collapse.

Show → Name → Explain → Implication: In 2020, Mastercard's risk analytics team built a modular "trust layer" for its global transaction network. Each new fraud-detection model was required to pass through a *value specification store*, a database that codified organisational commitments: fairness thresholds, privacy parameters, jurisdictional compliance rules. The next component, a *constraint solver,* continuously tested live model outputs against those specifications. A *harm monitor* observed emergent correlations—such as disproportionate transaction declines by merchant category or geography—and triggered human review when limits were breached. Finally, an *audit logger* captured decision rationales in real time, producing a tamper-evident record for regulators.

Within the first six months of deployment, Mastercard reported a 9% reduction in false-positive transaction blocks for small and minority-owned merchants (Mastercard AI Governance Report, 2021). Developers benefited from faster compliance approvals; auditors gained a transparent trail. Ethics had become not a governance bottleneck but a software feature.

This architecture reflects a design philosophy drawn from systems engineering: modularity as moral clarity. Each component answers a distinct question. The *value spec store* asks, "What do we care about?" The *constraint solver* asks, "Do our actions respect that care?" The *harm monitor* asks, "What new harms are we creating?" And the *audit logger* asks, "Can we prove it?" Together, they form a feedback loop that bridges aspiration and execution.

The counter-example is illuminating. In 2019, a major social media platform (publicly unnamed in the U.K. Parliamentary Committee Report, 2020) launched an automated content moderation model without integrated constraint testing. Its classifiers disproportionately flagged posts from regional dialect speakers as "spam" due to biased training data. When public backlash forced an internal review, engineers found no unified audit trail: ethical oversight was fragmented across spreadsheets, emails, and Jira tickets. The result was paralysis. Unlike Adyen or Mastercard, this firm had treated ethics as peripheral documentation rather than infrastructure. The contrast is not moral superiority—it is architectural competence.

Architecture is destiny. When ethics lives as code, accountability becomes routine. When it remains manual, it becomes theatre.

Interfaces, not principles, determine whether moral architecture endures. The Ethics Engine succeeds only when its tools speak fluently to both developers and auditors. For engineers, interfaces must be *integrated*—exposed as APIs, dashboards, and alerts that fit seamlessly into CI/CD workflows. For auditors, they must be *interpretable*—able to render complex model decisions in human-readable narratives.

A vivid example comes from Google's *Model Cards* framework (Mitchell et al., 2019). Originally conceived as a documentation tool, it evolved into a live interface within TensorFlow pipelines. Each model version automatically generates a card detailing dataset provenance, known limitations, and fairness evaluation results. These cards serve developers by providing contextual memory and regulators by providing evidence. In mature organisations, they form the front-end of the audit logger—the part of the Ethics Engine that translates computation into conscience.

Such interfaces close the gap between speed and scrutiny. At fintech firm Wise (formerly TransferWise), every model deployment triggers a dual-view dashboard: one for operational performance (latency, accuracy, throughput), another for ethical compliance (bias deltas, data provenance, incident flags). When a discrepancy emerges—for instance, a spike in false declines by customer segment—the deployment halts automatically. Engineers can override it, but only after logging a justification. The override log becomes part of the permanent audit trail. This coupling of autonomy and accountability converts ethical reflection into a daily engineering act.

Yet architecture alone cannot guarantee virtue. As every engineer knows, systems drift. Interfaces can decay into ritual, where buttons are clicked and boxes ticked without comprehension. The danger is *ethical drift*—the slow normalisation of exceptions. To counter it, high-reliability organisations, such as aviation or nuclear power, rely on *redundancy*: multiple overlapping systems of verification. The Ethics Engine must mirror this. A harm monitor must feed not only into internal dashboards but into independent review layers—compliance, risk, even external auditors. The system must design for inspection, not trust.

Some institutions are experimenting with this layered model. The Monetary Authority of Singapore's Veritas initiative (2022) provides open-source governance templates for AI in financial services. Its design pattern divides the ethics infrastructure into two planes: *in-line* controls embedded in model pipelines, and *out-of-line* oversight tools that operate asynchronously. Together, they create both agility and accountability. The architecture's genius lies in its dual visibility: developers see constraints in code; auditors see commitments in context.

The motif of scaffolding returns. Just as a bridge distributes load through its trusses, ethical architecture distributes accountability through interfaces. The structure matters less than the forces it channels. If too rigid, innovation stalls; if too loose, integrity collapses. The craft is in calibration.

A revealing limitation emerges in the open-source domain. Many fairness and interpretability libraries—such as IBM's AI Fairness 360 or Microsoft's Fairlearn—are technically sound but poorly adopted. Why? They lack seamless integration into CI/CD pipelines. Ethics becomes an optional post-processing step, detached from velocity. By contrast, companies that embed ethical checks directly into build and test stages—LinkedIn's *Fairness Toolkit* (2021), for example—achieve sustained impact. Their key insight: ethics must run *at runtime*.

This distinction between *real-time* and *retroactive* ethics mirrors a broader cultural shift. Retrospective review satisfies compliance; real-time constraint checking satisfies conscience. The latter prevents harm before it occurs, not after it's reported. The architectural principle is simple:

moral computation must operate on the same clock speed as machine learning.

A deeper implication follows. As ethics becomes software, it inherits software's virtues—and its vices. Modularity allows flexibility; it also permits selective blindness. An organisation can technically comply by implementing the audit logger but ignore the harm monitor. The only defence is *interface transparency*: when all components communicate through shared schemas and reporting pipelines, partial ethics becomes visible. Transparency, in this sense, is not disclosure but interoperability.

We can glimpse this future in regulatory alignment efforts. The European Union's AI Act (expected 2025) proposes "technical documentation obligations" requiring traceable model lifecycle data. This effectively mandates an Ethics Engine architecture: logged decisions, traceable constraints, auditable harm monitoring. Organisations that already treat ethics as software will adapt with minimal friction. Those that treat it as narrative will scramble. Regulation, in this case, rewards design discipline.

Architecture and interface are therefore not metaphors; they are the material through which ethical reasoning becomes executable. The Ethics Engine is less a product than a pattern—a way of building that recognises moral complexity as a systems property, not a managerial one. It demands collaboration across roles: engineers, ethicists, lawyers, and auditors share not a table but a terminal.

Yet the unresolved question lingers like background hum: can morality truly be modularised? Can compassion run at the speed of code? The best architectures do not pretend to answer definitively. They accept the imperfection of translation but build regardless. The value lies not in perfection but in persistence—in the scaffolding that keeps human judgment upright under the weight of automation.

The diagnostic question for any organisation, then, is simple: when your next model deploys, where does its conscience run? In a slide deck—or in the pipeline itself? The answer reveals whether ethics is still decoration or, at last, design.

Patterns and Anti-Patterns

At 2:07 a.m. on 14 September 2020, engineers at Netflix's Los Gatos campus pushed a silent update to their recommendation algorithm. For twelve hours, the change ran invisibly alongside the production system—a *shadow deploy*. Every user interaction was mirrored, every ranking decision compared. The update never touched a live user, but its impact was fully measurable. By midday, analysts knew the result: the new model delivered a 6.4% improvement in engagement while reducing skew towards niche content categories. The deployment passed not because it was clever, but because it was *patterned*. The team had followed a proven sequence—shadow deploy, gated rollout, post-analysis, commit. Reliability was not heroism; it was choreography.

Patterns like this define mature engineering cultures. They are codified wisdom—shortcuts to good judgment. They exist so that moral vigilance does not rely on individual brilliance or memory. In high-stakes systems, repetition saves lives as much as innovation does. The aviation industry's devotion to the pre-flight checklist, a discipline pioneered after the 1935 Boeing Model 299 crash, turned fatal complexity into procedural safety. In ethical engineering, patterns play a parallel role: they turn fragile virtue into repeatable design.

The motif here is *muscle memory*. Ethical resilience, like safety, depends less on aspiration than on routine. The question is not whether an organisation knows what "doing the right thing" looks like, but whether it can perform it under pressure—when deadlines loom, alerts flash, or reputational risk spikes. Muscle memory, once built, becomes invisible until it is needed.

Show → Name → Explain → Implication: In 2018, Google's "Project Strobe" audit revealed that hundreds of external developers had broad access to Gmail user data through unreviewed APIs. Rather than freezing innovation outright, Google responded by institutionalising a *gated rollout* pattern for new data-sharing features. Each stage—design, implementation, user consent—was accompanied by automated privacy compliance checks. The process replaced blanket trust with graduated confidence. Within a year, user complaints about unauthorised data access had dropped by 80% (Google Transparency Report, 2019). The lesson was architectural, but also moral: constraints can accelerate progress when they are predictable.

Contrast that with a classic anti-pattern: the *post-freeze review*. In 2021, a major autonomous vehicle company (documented in NTSB preliminary reports) delayed ethical risk assessments until after software "freezes"—the point at which changes were discouraged. When a fatal pedestrian accident occurred in Arizona, internal audits revealed that safety evaluators had identified the hazard months earlier but lacked authority to stop the build. The process guaranteed failure: it privileged schedule over conscience. Post-freeze reviews resemble moral archaeology—valuable for learning, useless for prevention.

Between these extremes lies the work of pattern-building: creating reusable solutions for recurring moral failures. *Red-team drills*, drawn from cybersecurity practice, provide one such pattern. In 2022, Anthropic, the AI research firm, adopted structured "ethical red-teaming" to probe its language models for manipulation and bias. The process—simulating adversarial misuse before release—produced quantifiable results. Its GPT-like model passed 14% more safety checks after each round (Anthropic Research Notes, 2023). More importantly, the exercise changed posture: engineers began to see ethical testing as part of design, not defence.

Patterns persist because they convert learning into reflex. They demand institutional humility—the recognition that no one is above process. When the U.K.'s National Health

Service began using algorithmic triage tools during the COVID-19 pandemic, it embedded a *shadow validation* step. Each new predictive model ran alongside human triage decisions for three weeks before deployment. The result was measurable: error variance decreased by 23%, and false negatives—missed high-risk patients—fell sharply (NHS AI Lab Evaluation, 2021). These gains did not come from better algorithms but from disciplined procedure. The moral pattern was patience.

Still, patterns alone can decay into bureaucracy. The temptation is to codify without questioning. Aviation's checklist revolution, which began as liberation, later faced its own anti-pattern: *checkbox fatigue*. Pilots, overwhelmed by rote tasks, began skipping steps under pressure. Only when airlines introduced *dynamic checklists*—responsive to flight conditions—did compliance rebound. The parallel in technology ethics is clear. Ethical checklists must evolve with context; otherwise, they become moral deadweight.

The anti-pattern of *ownerless metrics* illustrates this risk vividly. In 2019, several social platforms implemented "well-being scores" to track user harm. Metrics were defined but never assigned to accountable teams. When quarterly reviews came, no one could explain deteriorating scores, and incentives favoured engagement growth instead. Ethical measurement without ownership becomes moral theatre: data that informs nobody, decisions that change nothing. By contrast, organisations such as Microsoft's Responsible AI Office assign each metric—bias rate, appeal turnaround, harm incidence—to named stewards. When responsibility is personal, numbers regain meaning.

Checklists, in this context, are not paperwork but *scaffolds of consistency*. Boeing's original 1935 checklist had four lines; modern aerospace checklists run to hundreds of items. Yet the principle remains: prevent oversight through memory externalisation. Ethical engineering checklists follow the same logic. They might include pre-launch fairness validation, post-incident reporting cadence, and consent verification. What matters is not the content but the discipline of repetition. Every ethical failure ever analysed—from algorithmic bias to data breach—has its counterpart in a missed step.

A telling example of checklist success comes from the U.S. Air Force's "Operational Risk Management" (ORM) model, standardised in 1996. Each mission plan includes a five-step checklist—identify, assess, decide, implement, and supervise risk. When adapted to AI model deployment at Lockheed Martin's Skunk Works division in 2020, this same framework reduced critical post-deployment incidents by 30% over twelve months. The pattern's durability across decades and domains demonstrates a truth: ethics, like safety, is transferable through disciplined repetition.

The motif of *muscle memory* returns here. Patterns are the organisational equivalent of reflex arcs. They allow systems to react correctly before deliberation catches up. Yet reflexes require training. Teams must *rehearse* ethical procedures under simulated stress—just as pilots practise engine failures or hospitals stage disaster drills. Without rehearsal, even the best patterns wither.

But patterns can also be weaponised. The danger lies in ritualised process as alibi. After the 2017 Equifax breach, executives pointed to extensive "security procedures" that had been followed. The failure, investigators found, was not procedural omission but procedural blindness: patches were applied to test environments but never production. The pattern existed; it simply insulated complacency. The implication is sobering: a pattern library without introspection can become an archive of excuses.

To avoid that fate, organisations must treat pattern libraries as living documents. At Spotify, the internal "Golden Path" system—documenting preferred engineering patterns—is continuously updated based on incident reports and post-mortems. In 2021, the ethics and safety teams began adding moral design patterns alongside technical ones: fairness-aware rollout gates, human-in-the-loop escalation templates, consent prompt flows. By integrating ethical patterns into the same platform that manages technical patterns, Spotify made them part of everyday engineering grammar. Moral reflex became technical habit.

There is, however, a structural limitation worth naming. Patterns thrive in environments with stable context. When technology or regulation shifts too quickly—such as in generative AI or quantum security—yesterday's pattern can encode tomorrow's harm. The reconciliation is adaptability:

patterns must be versioned like code. Every pattern should include sunset clauses or review triggers. Ethical permanence lies not in preservation but in renewal.

Consistency replacing heroics is the moral axis of mature engineering. Heroism may solve crises, but it cannot scale. When an organisation depends on moral heroes, failure is only one absence away. Patterns replace dependence with design. They make ethics reproducible, testable, and improvable. They turn conscience from personality into protocol.

Yet the open question remains: how do we preserve imagination once procedure dominates? Every checklist risks narrowing vision; every pattern risks discouraging dissent. If ethics becomes too patterned, creativity suffocates. If too free, chaos returns. The forward test, then, is balance. When your next ethical failure occurs—and it will—ask not only "Which pattern failed?" but "Which pattern should never have existed?" The courage to retire bad patterns may be the highest form of ethical design.

Tooling the Workflow

On 17 February 2022, at Meta's London office, a fairness audit stalled the rollout of a new advertising model by forty-eight hours. The cause was mundane: a documentation pipeline had failed to generate an interpretability report for one of the feature sets. But the outcome was consequential. Without that single document—an automatically generated model card containing bias metrics and decision logic—the model could not be approved for deployment. Within minutes, engineers had traced the issue to a missing metadata tag in the fairness library's configuration file. The pipeline was patched, rerun, and approved. What mattered was not the glitch but the governance: the workflow itself had enforced ethics as a technical dependency.

That scene encapsulates a shift underway across advanced engineering organisations: ethics is becoming *operational code*. Where earlier generations treated fairness, transparency, and accountability as human oversight tasks, mature teams now encode them into their continuous integration and deployment (CI/CD) environments. Documentation, interpretability, and fairness tools are no longer decorative appendages—they are executable commitments. The moral dimension of software development, once confined to committees and compliance teams, now runs on version control.

The motif of this section is *instrumentation*. Just as precision instruments revolutionised science by making invisible forces measurable, modern tooling makes ethical quality observable. Ethics, properly tooled, becomes data—visible, testable, improvable. Without instruments, even the most eloquent ethical principles remain abstract. With them, conscience enters the workflow.

Show → Name → Explain → Implication: In 2018, Google introduced *Model Cards for Model Reporting* (Mitchell et al., 2019), an open framework for documenting machine-learning models. Each card automatically summarises a model's purpose, dataset composition, performance across subgroups, and known limitations. Integrated into TensorFlow Extended, these cards are generated as part of build pipelines, not after the fact. By 2020, internal audits showed that projects using automated documentation reported 60% faster compliance reviews and significantly fewer post-deployment bias incidents. The card system succeeded because it embedded reflection into process, not process into reflection.

Documentation, however, is only one instrument. Interpretability tools—those that reveal how models make decisions—bridge the gap between statistical output and human accountability. In 2017, Microsoft released *InterpretML,* an open-source library for explainable AI. Its deployment at JPMorgan Chase's credit scoring systems (reported in 2021) allowed regulators to inspect feature contributions at transaction-level granularity. When a model's rejections disproportionately affected small-business loan applicants, engineers identified a subtle proxy variable linked to postal codes. The feature was pruned, and approval fairness improved by 14%. The interpretability pipeline turned an ethical question—*why did this model decide this way?*—into an engineering artefact.

Fairness tools extend this logic to measurement. IBM's *AI Fairness 360* (2018) introduced over seventy bias detection metrics—statistical parity difference, equalised odds, disparate impact ratio—allowing teams to quantify harm before it occurs. Singapore's Government Technology Agency applied the toolkit in its citizen-services recommender systems in 2021, identifying gender imbalance in digital service visibility. By incorporating fairness audits into CI/CD gating logic, the agency reduced skew without slowing deployment. The implication is clear: fairness tooling works when it lives inside the workflow, not as an afterthought to it.

But tools can also betray their promise. A counter-example illustrates the trap. Between 2019 and 2020, several Fortune 500 firms adopted commercial "AI ethics dashboards" marketed as turnkey governance platforms. Independent evaluations by ForHumanity (2021) found that many of these tools lacked integration APIs or custom audit hooks. They visualised fairness metrics but could not influence model behaviour. In short, they *decorated decks* rather than *informed decisions*. The organisations acquired shelfware—expensive dashboards admired but unused. The failure was not technological but procedural: procurement teams bought tools for optics, not operations.

The tension between open-source and vendor solutions lies at the heart of this dilemma. Open-source tools like Fairlearn or SHAP offer transparency, adaptability, and community validation—but demand internal expertise. Vendor products promise enterprise support, liability coverage, and board-ready reporting—but risk opacity and dependence. Mature teams navigate this trade-off candidly. The Monetary Authority of Singapore's Veritas Consortium

(2022) adopted a hybrid approach: open-source fairness modules for transparency, vendor platforms for scale and auditability. Their insight: trust grows from hybrid architectures, not ideological purity.

The procurement process itself becomes an ethical act. Every tool purchase signals an organisation's philosophy of accountability. In 2021, the European Commission's Directorate-General for Informatics implemented procurement criteria that required vendors of AI systems to provide full model documentation, reproducibility scripts, and bias audit trails. The result was paradoxical: fewer vendors qualified, but integration efficiency improved. Procurement, when properly designed, is governance by other means.

The motif of instrumentation deepens here. Ethical instrumentation requires calibration—knowing what the dials mean. A fairness metric is meaningless without interpretive context. In 2020, researchers at the Alan Turing Institute analysed the use of bias metrics in public-sector AI systems and found widespread metric misuse: teams optimised for statistical parity even when demographic data were incomplete. The tool was sound; the interpretation was flawed. This underscores the central truth of tooling ethics: instruments must be matched by literacy. A dashboard can visualise bias, but only trained judgment can resolve it.

Documentation acts as connective tissue across the ethics engine. When every model carries a living document—

versioned, searchable, and auditable—organisations gain *memory*. This memory prevents drift. When a new engineer joins or a regulator audits, the rationale for each design choice is discoverable. Meta's *Responsible AI Index*, launched in 2022, links model cards, data sheets, and fairness reports into a single traceable graph. The internal finding: transparency reduced duplicated work by 27% across teams and accelerated ethics reviews by weeks. Documentation, often derided as bureaucratic, proved to be moral infrastructure.

A practical limitation deserves honesty. Tooling cannot guarantee virtue; it can only surface signals. Interpretability tools often trade clarity for completeness—simple explanations may mislead. Fairness metrics can conflict: one group's statistical parity may violate another's predictive equality. Documentation can ossify bad assumptions if not periodically revisited. These are not arguments against tooling, but warnings against complacency. Instruments magnify what exists—they cannot create conscience where none resides.

Still, when combined with cultural commitment, the tools alter the physics of decision-making. Consider the *ethics gate* pattern used at DeepMind since 2021. Every model deployment passes through an automated pre-launch checklist that runs documentation validation, fairness audits, and interpretability verification. The gate produces a binary signal: deploy or block. Each block requires human override, recorded with rationale. Over twelve months, ethics gate blocks accounted for 3% of deployment delays but prevented at least two major reputational incidents. The measurable trade-off was small; the moral dividend large.

The most sophisticated systems treat tooling as a dialogue, not a decree. At Spotify, the "Responsible ML Toolkit" integrates open-source explainability libraries with proprietary dashboards that collect qualitative annotations from developers. Each anomaly—a bias flag, a low-confidence region—prompts engineers to record reasoning. The act of annotation becomes ethical rehearsal, transforming the workflow into a site of learning. The outcome is not compliance but awareness.

The risk of *shelfware* remains ever-present. Tools purchased without integration plans decay into static optics. In 2023, an audit by PwC found that 64% of firms claiming to use "AI ethics tooling" had no metrics indicating deployment impact. Tooling, like instrumentation, demands maintenance. Without regular calibration—feedback loops between detection, decision, and correction—the system reverts to noise. The most ethical tools, paradoxically, are those that *force* conversation rather than automate it away.

The future trajectory of ethical tooling may lie in *self-explaining systems*: architectures where interpretability and fairness are native properties, not add-ons. In emerging frameworks such as Microsoft's *OpenAI Responsible Deployment Stack* (2024 pilot), documentation, monitoring, and audit functions interweave directly into the model's runtime. Every prediction carries its lineage; every anomaly its rationale. If successful, this would dissolve the boundary between ethics and engineering entirely.

Yet the unresolved question persists: when ethics becomes automated, who remains accountable? If a fairness gate blocks deployment, is the gate's creator responsible—or the engineer whose model triggered it? The paradox of tooling is that it distributes judgment even as it obscures authorship. The diagnostic test for any organisation, then, is simple: when a tool flags a moral conflict, who acts? If the answer is "no one," the workflow has failed, no matter how instrumented it appears.

The ethics of automation, ultimately, depend on more than code. Tools can measure, monitor, and memorialise—but they cannot care. Their virtue lies in design; their integrity, in use. The goal is not to automate conscience but to scaffold it—to make moral awareness as continuous, traceable, and operational as the systems it governs. The question that remains for every builder is whether their tools illuminate or anaesthetise. The difference is the measure of their ethics.

From Pilot to Policy

At 8:15 a.m. on 7 April 2021, the board of the Dutch bank ING convened in Amsterdam to review an unusual line item in its quarterly report: *ethical model audit expenditure*. The figure was small—just €480,000—but the discussion it triggered reshaped the bank's AI governance architecture. The pilot behind it had begun as a modest experiment: embedding a fairness check into credit-risk models for SME loans. Six months later, after a demonstrable 5% improvement in approval parity across gender and geography, the pilot had matured into an institutional mandate. The budget line became permanent. A board-level subcommittee for algorithmic accountability was formed. What had started as a single project now shaped how risk itself was defined and reported.

The episode illustrates how institutionalisation begins—not with grand declarations, but with small wins that prove measurable and repeatable. Ethics, when properly designed, is cumulative. The challenge is not invention but integration: how to transform scattered pilots, dashboards, and workshops into durable governance. The transition from pilot to policy marks the moment when moral ambition meets organisational metabolism. It is where values become budgets, training becomes routine, and accountability becomes systemic.

The motif running through this subchapter is *habit formation*. Just as muscles strengthen through repetition, ethical governance matures through iteration. The Ethics Engine cannot remain an innovation project; it must become infrastructure. And like any infrastructure, its survival depends less on rhetoric than on reinforcement—budgets, reporting cycles, and executive muscle memory.

Show → Name → Explain → Implication: When Microsoft formalised its *Responsible AI Standard* in 2022, it codified practices that had evolved through years of pilots—model cards, impact assessments, fairness gates—into binding corporate policy. Each new AI product was required to complete a "Responsible AI Impact Assessment" (RAI-A) before release, with findings reported to a cross-functional oversight committee. Over eighteen months, this process scaled across 300 teams, supported by internal training and budgeted compliance functions. The result was not only reduced ethical risk but improved product velocity: teams that followed the RAI-A process experienced 40% fewer post-launch issue escalations (Microsoft, 2023). The company's insight was simple: ethics scales when funded, not merely endorsed.

Budgeting anchors belief. Without explicit allocation, ethics dissolves into aspiration. In 2020, the OECD surveyed 200 organisations implementing AI ethics frameworks and found that 73% lacked dedicated funding lines. Unsurprisingly, fewer than 15% had sustained programs beyond pilot stage. The moral of the data is economic: virtue competes for resources. Institutionalising ethics means assigning cost centres, just as one does for cybersecurity or safety. ING's modest budget, Microsoft's global one—each signals legitimacy through permanence.

Yet money alone does not sustain momentum. Training transforms intent into capacity. Singapore's Government Technology Agency (GovTech) provides a case study in disciplined institutionalisation. In 2022, it launched *AI Verify*, a national framework combining technical testing and process audits. The pilot began with ten government systems; within a year, it became standard practice. Critical to the rollout was training: over 1,000 civil servants completed modules on interpretability, bias testing, and documentation. The result was cultural diffusion—ethical reasoning embedded in ordinary technical work. The program's architects understood that habits form not from policy statements, but from muscle repetition.

Contrast this with a cautionary example. In 2019, an international telecommunications firm launched an AI ethics taskforce following regulatory scrutiny. The initiative produced eloquent principles and glossy materials, but no operational tooling or reporting mechanisms. Within a year, leadership rotated, budgets lapsed, and the taskforce dissolved. The pilot had produced vocabulary, not velocity. The failure was diagnostic: institutionalisation cannot depend on personalities; it must depend on process.

Reporting closes the feedback loop. It turns the invisible—bias rates, audit outcomes, incident frequency—into visible governance. The best institutions treat reporting not as compliance theatre but as organisational introspection. At DeepMind, the *Safety and Ethics Review Committee* publishes internal summaries of model assessments to all employees. This transparency, rare in corporate settings, has a quantifiable effect: survey data from 2023 showed a 17% increase in employee confidence that ethical issues would be addressed seriously. Reporting, when open, builds credibility both inside and out.

The counter-example reveals the fragility of opacity. A major fintech, later fined by the U.K. Financial Conduct

Authority in 2022, had implemented an ethics committee without publishing its remit or outcomes. Employees assumed reviews were symbolic; compliance staff bypassed it under deadline pressure. The committee existed, but it was invisible, and therefore irrelevant. Policy without visibility is bureaucracy, not governance.

The bridge from pilot to policy is paved with *translation*: translating experimentation into standardisation, enthusiasm into accountability, and data into doctrine. That process is neither linear nor risk-free. As patterns repeat, novelty fades; fatigue sets in. Ethical enthusiasm can harden into procedural cynicism—the sense that "ethics" is just another box to tick. Here, leadership narrative matters. Executives who frame ethical governance as innovation, not inhibition, sustain engagement. In 2021, Salesforce's Chief Ethical and Humane Use Officer reframed bias mitigation pilots as "trust accelerators," linking them to revenue stability and customer retention metrics. The linguistic shift—ethics as enabler—preserved momentum and executive buy-in.

Board accountability anchors continuity. When oversight becomes a fiduciary obligation rather than a moral preference, ethics survives turnover. The Bank of England's 2023 supervisory guidance explicitly requires boards to demonstrate understanding of algorithmic risk, including fairness and explainability. Board minutes now capture not only financial risk but ethical risk appetite. The implication is profound: moral reasoning has entered corporate governance architecture. Ethics is no longer soft power; it is statutory duty.

The motif of habit deepens here. Institutions mature when routines absorb principle. The United Nations Development Programme's 2022 *AI Ethics Framework for the Global South* demonstrated this with its "policy pipeline" model. Each pilot project—say, a health data initiative in Kenya or an agricultural analytics system in India—had to include three closing artefacts: a lessons-learned report, a training module, and a budget proposal for continuation. This discipline ensured that successful pilots became templates, not trophies. By the program's second year, forty-eight projects had evolved into formal policies across seven countries. The process proved that institutionalisation is not bureaucracy—it is memory.

Still, institutionalisation carries risk. Routinisation can erode vigilance. A 2023 audit of several European AI ethics programs found that, after initial success, many devolved into compliance checklists detached from real decision-making. The antidote is periodic disruption: rotating auditors, inviting external review, or staging ethical "fire drills." Continuity must be balanced by freshness. The muscle must not only remember; it must adapt.

The question of *scale* arises inevitably. How large must the ethics engine become before it chokes on its own weight? Over-centralisation can breed delay; over-delegation can breed inconsistency. The most effective structures, like those at the BBC or the Monetary Authority of Singapore, use federated models: a central ethics team sets standards, while embedded liaisons in product teams handle implementation. This hybrid design maintains coherence without stifling agility. Governance becomes distributed muscle, not central nervous control.

What distinguishes institutions that sustain ethics from those that don't is *closure of the loop*. Pilots begin the conversation; policies end it by encoding learning into infrastructure. Every model deployment, every post-mortem, every audit feeds back into training, budgeting, and reporting. Over time, this feedback cycle generates resilience. The Ethics Engine becomes not an innovation but a reflex. Its activation no longer depends on crisis; it hums quietly beneath normal operations.

And yet, a question persists like a quiet undertone: can ethics ever truly become habit without losing consciousness? Habit is efficiency, but morality demands reflection. The challenge of institutionalisation is to preserve awareness within automation—to keep the moral muscle awake even as it strengthens. When an organisation's ethics engine runs smoothly, someone must still ask whether it remembers why it runs at all. That question, uncomfortable yet vital, is the final test of maturity.

About the Author

Levent Karaman writes at the seam where code meets conscience. Raised between workshop pragmatism and library philosophy, he builds systems that work in the world without forgetting the people in it. His work asks unfashionable questions—who is left out of the dataset, what duty outlives a deadline, where does a model's confidence exceed its right to decide—and answers them with artefacts you can ship: value specifications, harm tables, audit trails. He draws on a European inheritance of public reasoning, from Spinoza's realism about power to Mary Midgley's distrust of single big ideas, and pairs it with the builder's instinct to make ethics testable. Off the page he mentors product teams and community reviewers, believing good governance is a civic craft, not a compliance ritual. He writes to give practitioners language, tools, and courage enough to choose the slower good.

www.ingramcontent.com/pod-product-compliance
Lightning Source LLC
Chambersburg PA
CBHW031340230926
51848CB00002B/316
9789374126653